DEEP and SURFACE STRUCTURE CONSTRAINTS in SYNTAX

TRANSATLANTIC SERIES in LINGUISTICS
Under the general editorship of
Samuel R. Levin
Graduate Center
The City University
of New York

ANALYTIC SYNTAX
OTTO JESPERSEN

THE STUDY OF SYNTAX
The Generative-Transformational Approach
to the Structure of American English
D. TERENCE LANGENDOEN

INTRODUCTION TO TAGMEMIC ANALYSIS
WALTER A. COOK, S.J.

IRREGULARITY IN SYNTAX
GEORGE LAKOFF

CROSS-OVER PHENOMENA
PAUL M. POSTAL

DEEP and SURFACE STRUCTURE CONSTRAINTS in SYNTAX

DAVID M. PERLMUTTER

Massachusetts Institute of Technology

HOLT, RINEHART AND WINSTON, INC.
New York   Chicago   San Francisco   Atlanta
Dallas   Montreal   Toronto   London   Sydney

For my father and mother,
Victor and Fruma Perlmutter

To the Reader

Most of this book is written so as to be intelligible to someone who is acquainted with the most basic concepts of transformational grammar —deep structure, surface structure, and transformations. Knowledge of particular transformational rules and analyses is not presupposed. The only exception to this statement is Chapter 1, which is by far the most difficult. Since Chapter 1 is self-contained and is not prerequisite to understanding the rest of the book, the beginner should start with Chapter 2 and proceed to the end of the book, returning to Chapter 1 later on. If it is read in this way, this book can be read by students toward the end of their first semester of transformational grammar.

D. M. P.

Cambridge, Massachusetts
April 1971

Acknowledgments

I am deeply grateful to the many people who contributed in many different ways to the making of this book. Although I cannot mention them all individually, I would like to single out a few to whom I am especially indebted.

Of my teachers in linguistics, there are four who stand out. Noam Chomsky, Morris Halle, Paul Postal, and John Ross have each contributed something to my understanding of linguistics that I could have found in no one else. They have also contributed in many ways to the ideas and arguments in this book. Paul Postal and John Ross have also read much of the final manuscript and improved it by their suggestions.

Wayles Browne, Kenneth Hale, and James Harris have made their own contributions to the contents of this book. I have also benefited greatly from ideas and comments from Stephen Anderson, LeRoy Baker, George Bedell, Dwight Bolinger, Fred Householder, Richard Kayne, Jay Keyser, Susumu Kuno, S.-Y. Kuroda, George Lakoff, John Lyons, G. H. Matthews, Carlos Otero, and Brandon Qualls. Ljubivoje Aćimović, Claire Asselin, Ivonne Bordelois, Fortunato Danón, Carlos DeGregori, François Dell, Velimir Kuftinec, Denah Lida, Rastko Maglić, María-Luisa Rivero, Guillermo Segreda, and Jean-Roger Vergnaud have been of inestimable help with the data from their respective native languages. For help in reading proof I am indebted to Avery Andrews and Mary-Louise Kean. While all of these people have contributed materially to this book, responsibility for errors is mine alone.

I would like to thank D. Reidel Publishing Company and Librairie Larousse for permission to reprint those portions of this book that they have previously published.

The writing of this book was supported in part by the National Science Foundation through Grant No. GS-2005 to Brandeis University. Work done when I was a graduate student was supported in part by a graduate fellowship in linguistics from the American Council of Learned Societies.

D. M. P.

Introduction

This book is concerned primarily with the problem of filtering in generative grammar—the problem of generalized phrase markers generated by the base component that underlie no well-formed sentences, and the kinds of grammatical devices that are needed to characterize such sentences as ungrammatical.

Chapter 1 is concerned with certain nonsentences that have ill-formed deep structures whose ill formedness cannot be characterized by means of the blocking of an obligatory transformation. It is shown that there are certain verbs requiring that the subject of a sentence embedded beneath them be identical to their own subject, and there are other verbs requiring that the embedded subject be nonidentical to their own subject. These constraints, which I call *deep structure constraints,* are well-formedness conditions on generalized phrase markers that apply prior to the application of tranformations and "filter out" certain generalized phrase markers generated by the base as ill formed.

In Chapter 2, it is shown that in order to characterize certain Spanish sentences as ungrammatical, it is necessary to impose a *surface structure constraint* that acts as a filter and rejects as ungrammatical any sentence that contains object pronouns that are not in the prescribed order. It happens that in certain cases where the surface structure that results from a particular deep structure is rejected as ungrammatical by the surface structure constraint, there is no way to actualize that deep structure as a grammatical sentence. As a result, there are well-formed deep structures to which there corresponds no grammatical surface structure.

In Chapter 3, it is shown that the inclusion in linguistic theory of surface structure constraints of the kind motivated in Chapter 2 carries with it a specific prediction about the role of phonological information in syntax. Two examples of the predicted type are discussed.

Chapter 4 motivates a surface structure constraint in the grammars of French and English and contrasts them with languages that lack this constraint. It is suggested that languages differ typologically according to whether or not their grammars contain this surface structure constraint.

In sum, it is shown here that grammars must include deep structure constraints or well-formedness conditions on generalized phrase markers generated by the base component and surface structure constraints or well-formedness conditions on the output of the transformational component. This endows grammars with filtering devices at the levels of deep and surface structure in addition to the filtering function of transformations proposed in Noam Chomsky's *Aspects of the Theory of Syntax*. The availability of so many filtering devices makes grammars too powerful and therefore weakens linguistic theory, unless the availability of these filtering devices is used to constrain grammars in ways that were not possible in earlier theory. In the Epilogue, some tentative suggestions are put forth as to how the availability of surface structure constraints can contribute to the development of an evaluation measure for grammars, which by its very nature constrains the range of grammars allowed by linguistic theory and enriches linguistic theory correspondingly.

D. M. P.

Contents

DEEP and SURFACE STRUCTURE
CONSTRAINTS in SYNTAX

1 EVIDENCE FOR DEEP STRUCTURE CONSTRAINTS IN SYNTAX

0. THE PROBLEM

In *Aspects of the Theory of Syntax,* Chomsky proposed the introduction of contextual (strict subcategorizational and selectional) features into linguistic theory to specify the types of deep structures into which particular lexical items could be inserted. He also introduced into theory generalized phrase markers generated by recursive phrase structure rules of the base component capable of reintroducing the symbol S in deep structures any number of times. Each S would then be expanded further by the rewrite rules of the base. Lexical items would then be inserted into the generalized phrase markers produced in this way.

This theoretical framework gives rise to the question of whether the insertion of lexical items into generalized phrase markers will result in ill-formed deep structures, and what grammatical devices are necessary to prevent this. It was to state constraints on the distribution of a lexical item within a given simplex S that Chomsky proposed contextual features associated with the lexical item. No specific provisions were made in *Aspects* for constraints on lexical items extending across S boundaries within generalized phrase markers. Chomsky pointed out, however, that unconstrained [1] insertion of lexical items into generalized phrase markers would produce deep structures which underlie no well-formed sentences. Considering relative clauses, he pointed out that a relative clause must contain a noun phrase identical to the antecedent, and that unconstrained [1] insertion of lexical items into deep structures would give rise to deep structures in which this condition was not satisfied. Some device was needed to characterize such deep structures as ill-formed. Rather than introduce some kind

F. Kiefer (ed.), *Studies in Syntax and Semantics,* 168–186. © D. Reidel, Dordrecht-Holland.

[1] Unconstrained except for the constraints stated by means of contextual features.

of constraint on deep structures themselves, Chomsky proposed the device of transformational blocking of derivations. In the case of relative clauses which contain no noun phrase identical to the antecedent, the obligatory relativization transformation would "block" because the condition requiring two identical noun phrases would not be satisfied. The "blocking" of the derivation caused by the inability of this obligatory transformation to apply would characterize the sentence as ungrammatical. The notion "well-formed deep structure" thus was not defined solely in terms of constraints on deep structures themselves, but was a derivative notion, defined transformationally. Only those generalized phrase markers which passed through the transformational component with no transformations causing the derivation to "block" would qualify as deep structures. To quote Chomsky:

> Not all generalized Phrase-markers generated by the base will underlie actual sentences and thus qualify as deep structures. What, then, is the test that determines whether a generalized Phrase-marker is the deep structure of some sentence? The answer is very simple. The transformational rules provide exactly such a test, and there is, in general, no simpler test. A generalized Phrase-marker M_D is the deep structure underlying the sentence S, with the surface structure M_S, just in case the transformational rules generate M_S from M_D. The surface structure M_S of S is well formed just in case S contains no symbols indicating the blocking of obligatory transformations. A deep structure is a generalized Phrase-marker underlying some well-formed surface structure. Thus the basic notion defined by a transformational grammar is: *deep structure M_D underlies well-formed surface structure M_S*. The notion "deep structure" itself is derivative from this. The transformational rules act as a "filter" that permits only certain generalized Phrase-markers to qualify as deep structures.[2]

Given the framework of *Aspects,* Chomsky's proposal to characterize ill-formed deep structures with relative clauses as ungrammatical by means of transformational blocking of the derivation is well suited to the particular constraint under consideration. What is required is that some noun phrase in the relative clause be identical to the antecedent. The constraint, then, is not a property of any particular lexical items, and could not be handled by means of contextual features associated with lexical items. Second, the constraint is one that requires identity between two noun phrases. The contextual features introduced in *Aspects* referred to strict subcategorizational and selectional features of noun phrases, but not to identity between two noun phrases. This was, however, a condition found repeatedly in the statement of transformations. Since the relativization transformation had to require identity between the relativized noun phrase and the antecedent in any case, it seemed natural to make use of this requirement as a means of characterizing as ill formed any deep structure in which this requirement was not met.

---

[2] Chomsky (1965), 138–139.

It is the purpose of this chapter to show that there exist in natural languages ill-formed generalized phrase markers generated by the base component which cannot be characterized as such by means of the blocking of transformations. The data on which this conclusion is based comes from sentences which manifest identity or nonidentity constraints between the subjects of certain verbs and the subjects of their complements.[3] Two types of arguments are given to show that these constraints cannot be stated transformationally. One type of argument is based on the fact that if identity or nonidentity constraints on noun phrases are to be stated transformationally, the constraints must require that the relevant noun phrases be identical or nonidentical at the stage in derivations at which the relevant transformation applies. It is shown here that there are subject-subject constraints which cannot be stated in this way, for they are constraints on underlying rather than derived subjects. A second type of argument is based on cases where the subject of a verb and the subject of its complement must be identical, but there is no obligatory transformation which applies to such structures. In one such case the relevant transformation is optional, while in another there is no transformation in the language which states an identity condition between the two noun phrases which must be identical. There is therefore no transformation available that can be said to cause the derivation to "block." It is concluded that for both types of cases it is necessary to impose a constraint requiring identity (or nonidentity, as the case may be) of the subjects of certain verbs and the subjects of their complements prior to the application of transformations. We refer to these constraints as *deep structure constraints.*

The deep structure constraints proposed here go beyond the contextual features of *Aspects* in two respects. First, their domain extends beyond the boundaries of the simplex S in generalized phrase markers. Second, they refer crucially to identity and nonidentity of noun phrases. One could regard them as an extension of the device of contextual features introduced in *Aspects.* In this view, they would specify conditions on the insertion of particular verbs into deep structures. Within the framework of recent work in generative semantics, the constraints proposed here could likewise be viewed as conditions on lexical insertion. Alternatively, within either the *Aspects* theory or that of generative semantics one could view them as filters imposed on trees that already contain lexical items. In this view, their role would be that of discarding or filtering out ill-formed underlying structures. It is not clear at present whether there are any empirical differences among these differing views of the deep structure constraints proposed here, or whether they are merely notational variants. At any rate, we are not concerned here with differentiating among them. It is our purpose here only to show that the ill-formed structures in question can not be characterized as such by means of transformations.

---

3 We will also consider cases where the object of certain verbs must be identical to the subject of the complement sentence. In the discussion which follows we refer to subject-subject constraints, but always with the understanding that object-subject constraints are included.

1. THE UNLIKE-SUBJECT CONSTRAINT IN ENGLISH

In his study of complementation in English, Rosenbaum (1967) pointed out that in certain complement constructions the subject of the embedded sentence must be nonidentical to the subject of the matrix sentence.

(1)   I screamed for Clyde to commit himself.

(2)   a. *I screamed for me to commit myself.
           b. *I screamed to commit myself.

The question that concerns us here is one that lay beyond the scope of Rosenbaum's study—that of how such restrictions are to be stated in grammars.

The first attempt to state this restriction precisely was made by Lakoff (1965). Since the ill-formedness of *(2) is due not to any ill formedness of either simplex S by itself, but rather to the fact that a sentence with *I* as subject is embedded beneath the sentence *I screamed* with infinitival complementizer, Lakoff sought to account for the deviance of *(2) by extending Chomsky's proposal that it is the blocking of an obligatory transformation that "filters out" ill-formed generalized phrase markers as ungrammatical. In order to do this, Lakoff proposed the notion of "absolute exceptions" to transformational rules, marking the verb *scream* as an "absolute exception" to the rule of Equi-NP Deletion. This meant that *scream* had to be marked in the lexicon as requiring:

(a) that the structural description of Equi-NP Deletion *not* be met, and
(b) that Equi-NP Deletion *not* apply.

A verb marked only for (b) would be a "simple exception," in Lakoff's terminology. If *scream* were only a simple exception, however, *(2b) would be characterized as ungrammatical but *(2a) would not. The fact that *(2a) is ungrammatical as well led Lakoff to add requirement (a), making *scream* an "absolute exception" to the rule of Equi-NP Deletion. A violation would be registered in sentences with *scream,* marking the sentence as ungrammatical, in the event that the structural description of Equi-NP Deletion were met or in the event that the rule applied.

If one assumes that violations of grammaticality due to embedding of independently well-formed simplex S's in generalized phrase markers must be accounted for transformationally, one would be driven to some such notion as absolute exceptions. Since the constraint that accounts for the difference between (1) and *(2) requires nonidentity between the subject of a sentence and the subject of a sentence embedded beneath it, the only transformation we could possibly make use of to characterize the relevant sentences as ungrammatical would be a transformation that looks at the two subjects. The only transformation that does this is Equi-NP Deletion. The notion of absolute exceptions to Equi-NP Deletion, then, is a logical result of the attempt to account for the data transformationally.

There is a very simple way to test the correctness of this solution. If it is correct and the unlike-subject constraint is transformational in nature, then the grammaticality of the resulting sentence will depend on whether or not the subject of the embedded sentence and the matrix subject are non-identical *at the stage of derivations at which the Equi-NP Deletion transformation applies.* If, on the other hand, we are dealing with a deep structure constraint, then it is the identity or nonidentity of the two subjects before the application of any transformations that is relevant to the grammaticality or ungrammaticality of the resulting sentence. To decide between the two hypotheses, then, we must pick an example in which the embedded sentence no longer has the same subject when Equi-NP Deletion applies that it had in deep structure. One such example is:

(3) I screamed to be allowed to shave myself.

The deep structure of (3) is something like (4).[4]

(4)

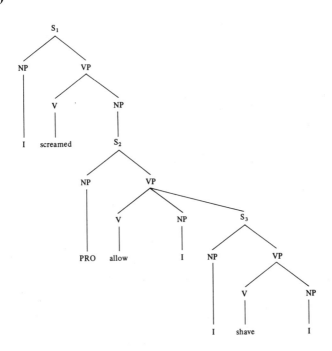

Reflexivization applies in S_3 on the first cycle, and on the second (S_2) cycle the subject of S_3 is deleted by Equi-NP Deletion and the passive transformation applies in S_2, so that *I* becomes the derived subject of S_2. After the second cycle, then, we have a derived structure like (5).

---

[4] All tree diagrams given here are highly oversimplified, ignoring any aspects of the tree that are not directly relevant to the points under discussion. For this reason such things

(5)

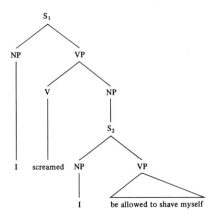

On the third (S_1) cycle, the (derived) subject of the sentence embedded beneath *scream* is in fact identical to the subject of *scream*. The structural description of Equi-NP Deletion is therefore met, and Equi-NP Deletion in fact applies. According to Lakoff's formalism, either of these two occurrences in the course of the derivation of a sentence with *scream* should cause the resulting sentence to be ungrammatical. But (3) is perfectly grammatical. We must conclude that this formalism is incorrect.

If, on the other hand, the unlike-subject constraint is a deep structure constraint, as proposed here, it does not matter whether or not the structural description of Equi-NP Deletion is met or the rule applies, as long as the subject of a sentence embedded beneath *scream* is not identical to the subject of *scream* in deep structure.[5] This condition is satisfied in (4), the struc-

---

as verb tense, auxiliary verbs, and complementizers are systematically ignored. The general framework is that of Chomsky (1965) and Rosenbaum (1967), but some changes have been made in the deep structures posited in those works. In particular, I am following Kiparsky and Kiparsky (1970) in omitting the *it* of noun phrase complements posited by Rosenbaum where they are not relevant to the points under discussion. Rosenbaum's "pronoun replacement transformation" is sometimes referred to here as "It-Replacement" and sometimes by the Kiparskys' term of "Raising." No justification is offered here either for the basic framework or for the modifications made in it, since nothing that is crucial to the argument developed here seems to hinge on these points.

5 Another way to test this hypothesis would be to consider a deep structure like (i). Here the subject of the sentence embedded beneath *scream* is identical to the subject of *scream* in deep structure. If the unlike-subject constraint is indeed a deep structure constraint, then this sentence should be ungrammatical no matter what happens in the course of its derivation. Using the notion of "absolute exception" to Equi-NP Deletion, on the other hand, the resulting sentence should be grammatical if the structural description of Equi-NP Deletion is not met and the rule does not apply. We can satisfy these two conditions in the following way. After Reflexivization has applied on the first (S_3)

(i)

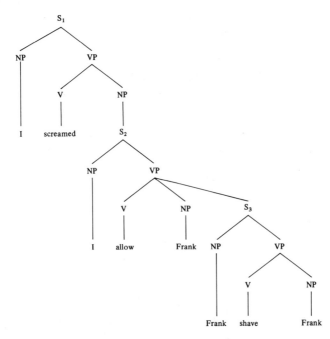

cycle and Equi-NP Deletion has deleted the subject *Frank* of S_3 on the second (S_2) cycle, let the passive transformation apply in S_2. This will yield a derived structure like (ii).

(ii)

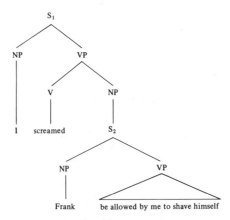

Now the (derived) subject of the sentence embedded beneath *scream* is nonidentical to the subject of *scream*, so that on the third (S_1) cycle, the structural description of Equi-NP Deletion is not met and the rule cannot and does not apply. According to Lakoff's formalism, the resulting sentence should be grammatical. But it is not:

ture underlying (3). The grammaticality of (3) is therefore evidence that the unlike-subject constraint is a deep structure constraint.[6]

It might be thought that a deep structure constraint like the unlike-subject constraint in English is essentially a "null transformation" which would require that the subject of a sentence embedded beneath verbs like *scream* be nonidentical to the subject of scream. But this constraint differs from a transformation not only in that it effects no change in phrase markers, but, more important, in that its "structural description" must be met if a grammatical sentence is to result. For this reason, the unlike-subject constraint is not like an obligatory transformation, which applies *if* its structural description is met, but it is rather a well-formedness condition on the input to the transformational component. To call it a "null transformation" is therefore to use the term "transformation" in an entirely new way. Furthermore, if well-formedness conditions on trees like the unlike-subject constraint were transformations, they could be ordered with respect to other

---

(iii) a. *I screamed for Frank to be allowed by me to shave himself.
     b. *I screamed for Frank to be allowed to shave himself by me.

If the unlike-subject constraint is a deep structure constraint, the ungrammaticality of *(iii) is correctly predicted, since the subject of S_2 is identical to the subject of S_1 in (i), the deep structure of *(iii). However, the validity of this argument is compromised by the fact (pointed out to me by John Ross) that regardless of whether or not the verb in the matrix sentence is an unlike-subject verb, in sentences in which the subject of the embedded sentence is identical to the subject of the matrix sentence, the passive transformation cannot apply in the embedded sentence without producing an ungrammatical sentence. If we substitute *expect* for *scream* in (i) and *(iii), then, the result is equally ungrammatical.

(iv) a. *I expected Frank to be allowed by me to shave himself.
     b. *I expected Frank to be allowed to shave himself by me.

[6] Note in passing that there are perfectly grammatical sentences with the verb *scream* in which the subject of the embedded sentence *is* identical to the subject of *scream* in deep structure. For example:

(v) I screamed that I would go.

The unlike-subject constraint is operative in sentences like (1) and *(2), but not in (v). We are therefore faced with the question of how to characterize this difference. At first glance, the difference between the two kinds of sentences appears to be due to the fact that (1) and *(2) have the infinitival complementizer, while (v) has the *that* complementizer. If this is the correct characterization of the difference between (1) and *(2), on the one hand, and (v), on the other, then the unlike-subject constraint must be restricted to sentences with the infinitival complementizer. If complementizers are present in deep structure, then this fact would not run counter to any claim that the unlike-subject constraint must be stated at the level of deep structure. A promising line of investigation for anyone desirous of disputing such a claim would be to show that sentences in which a complement is embedded beneath *scream* with the infinitival complementizer are themselves derived from "deeper" underlying structures. This would open up the possibility that the unlike-subject constraint is in fact a constraint on the transformation which introduces the infinitival complementizer in a subset of *scream* sentences with complements. We will not follow up this line of investigation here. It suffices here to have pointed out that the unlike-subject constraint does not apply to every sentence with a verb having the phonological shape *scream*.

transformations. This would be an exceedingly powerful device, since such filters could be applied at any stage of derivations. However, it seems that we can constrain this filtering device and claim that they are to be applied only to phrase markers which constitute the *input* to the transformational component.[7] For this reason we call the device that is needed to state the unlike-subject constraint in English a deep structure constraint.

2. THE LIKE-SUBJECT CONSTRAINT IN SERBO-CROATIAN

Rosenbaum (1967) pointed out that in certain complement constructions in English, the subject of the embedded sentence must be identical to the subject of the matrix sentence. This is the case with the verb *condescend,* so that

(6) I condescended to commit myself.

is grammatical, but

(7) *I condescended (for) Bill to commit himself.

is not. In examples of transitive verb phrase complementation, the subject of the embedded sentence must be identical to the object of the matrix sentence.

(8) I forced Fred to commit himself.

(9) *I forced Fred (for) Roxanne to commit herself.

Lakoff (1965), extending Chomsky's suggestion that ill-formed generalized phrase markers be characterized as such by the blocking of an obligatory transformation, proposed that the verbs *condescend* and *force* be marked in the lexicon as "absolute exceptions" to the rule of Equi-NP Deletion, requiring that the structural description of Equi-NP Deletion be met and that the transformation actually apply. In this section, we shall see that there are identity constraints of exactly the same kind in Serbo-Croatian. In Serbo-Croatian, however, the rule of Equi-NP Deletion is optional in the case of subject-subject identity, while in the case of object-subject identity Equi-NP Deletion does not apply at all.[8] There is therefore no obligatory transformation whose failure to apply (and to have its structural description met) we can use to characterize as ungrammatical those sentences in which

---

7 Surface structure constraints, another class of such filtering devices, are discussed in the last three chapters of this book.

8 Some speakers accept sentences like

    (vi)   Pomagao sam mu graditi kuću.
           'I helped him build the house.'

in which the subject of the embedded sentence has been deleted upon identity with the (Dative) object of the matrix sentence. For this reason it is an oversimplification to say that there is no Equi-NP Deletion dependent on identity to the matrix object in Serbo-Croatian. Nonetheless, this statement is true of most cases of transitive verb phrase complementation in Serbo-Croatian, as it is of the cases to be examined here.

the identity constraint is not met. We shall see that to characterize such sentences of Serbo-Croatian as ungrammatical it is necessary to introduce deep structure constraints into linguistic theory.

In Serbo-Croatian, an embedded sentence may be introduced by the complementizer *da* in sentences like

(10)   a. Želim da idem.
           'I want that I go: I want to go.'
       b. Želim da ideš.
           'I want that you go: I want you to go.'
       c. Želim da Rastko ide.
           'I want that Rastko go: I want Rastko to go.'

There is also an infinitival complementizer. Serbo-Croatian does not have an "accusative plus infinitive" construction, and the distribution of the infinitival complementizer is much more restricted than that of the *da* complementizer. Whereas *da* occurs in full paradigms like (10), we may use the infinitival complementizer only in the realization of the deep structure underlying (10a). Its use in sentences like (10b) and (10c) results in ungrammaticality:

(11)   a. Želim ići.
           'I want to go.'
       b. *Želim te ići.
           'I want you to go.'
       c. *Želim Rastka ići.
           'I want Rastko to go.'

In a paradigm in which the verb *željeti* 'want' has a second person singular subject we find:

(12)   a. *Želiš me ići.
           'You want me to go.'
       b. Želiš ići.
           'You want to go.'
       c. *Želiš Rastka ići.
           'You want Rastko to go.'

The appearance of the infinitival complementizer, then, is predictable: it can occur only in sentences in which the subject of the embedded sentence is identical to the subject of the matrix sentence. The subject of the embedded sentence must have been deleted in order for the infinitival complementizer to appear, for the embedded subject never shows up together with the infinitival complementizer.

We can capture these generalizations by positing an optional rule of Equi-NP Deletion in Serbo-Croatian that deletes the subject of an embedded sentence if it is identical to the subject of the matrix sentence. In just those cases in which the subject of the embedded sentence has been deleted by Equi-NP Deletion will the embedded sentence be reduced to an infinitive. It is in this way that the infinitival complementizer will be intro-

duced. In this I am following Kiparsky and Kiparsky (1970), who have
proposed a similar analysis for English.[9]

[9] The situation is somewhat more complicated in English, since in English there is also
a rule of Raising or It-Replacement which takes an NP out of the embedded sentence
and moves it up into the higher sentence. This rule converts structures like (vii) to
structures like (viii), yielding sentences like (ix).

(vii)

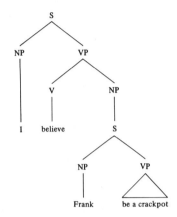

(viii)

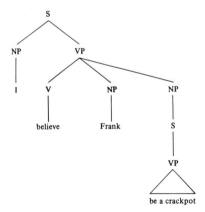

    (ix)   I believe Frank to be a crackpot.

That the NP *Frank* is indeed moved up into the higher sentence can be seen from
such examples as

    (x)   I believe myself to be a crackpot.

where the reflexive pronoun *myself* could not have arisen if the subject *I* of the embedded sentence had not been moved up into the higher sentence, since, as Lees and

This analysis squares with the facts of verb agreement in Serbo-Croatian. In sentences with the *da* complementizer the embedded verb is inflected to agree with its subject. (10a) derives from a structure like [10]

(13)

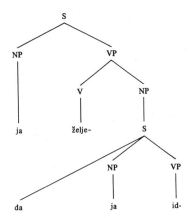

želje- and *id-* will now be inflected to agree with their subjects—*ja* in both cases. This will yield

(14) Ja želim da ja idem.
'I want that I go.'

Similarly, at this stage of derivations (10b) and (10c) are

(15) a. Ja želim da ti ideš.
'I want that you go.'
b. Ja želim da Rastko ide.
'I want that Rastko go.'

The embedded subjects *ja, ti,* and *Rastko* trigger verb agreement, so that the embedded verbs *idem, ideš,* and *ide* agree with their subjects *ja, ti,* and *Rastko* respectively. These inflected verb forms therefore testify to the presence of *ja, ti,* and *Rastko* in their respective sentences. At a later stage

---

Klima (1963) have shown, Reflexivization in English must be limited to a single simplex sentence in order to prevent such ungrammatical sentences as

(xi) *I believe Bill to have insulted myself.

Now, the appearance of the infinitive in sentences like (ix) and (x) does not run counter to the Kiparskys' proposal, since the correct generalization is that the infinitive appears whenever the subject NP has been removed from the embedded sentence during the course of a derivation, regardless of whether the subject NP has been removed by a deletion rule, such as Equi-NP Deletion, or by a movement rule, such as Raising. Nevertheless, there are occurrences of the infinitival complementizer in English which cannot be accounted for in this way. One such case is discussed in Chapter Four.

[10] These verbs are represented in tree diagrams as *želje-* and *id-* so as to be neutral between their inflected and infinitival forms.

in derivations, all nonemphatic subject pronouns in Serbo-Croatian are deleted. At this point, (14), (15a), and (15b) are converted into (10a), (10b), and (10c) respectively. Now, we have postulated that in sentences with the *da* complementizer in surface structure, Equi-NP Deletion has not taken place. The fact that in (10a) the embedded verb *idem* is inflected to agree with its subject *ja* supports this, since *ja* had to be present in order to trigger verb agreement. We hypothesized that the embedded infinitive results when the subject of the embedded sentence has been deleted by Equi-NP Deletion. In these cases the embedded verb is the infinitive *ići,* which is invariant in form. The lack of agreement on the infinitive squares with our hypothesis, which entails that since the subject of the embedded sentence has been deleted by Equi-NP Deletion, there is no subject for it to agree with. The fact that the embedded verb agrees with its subject in embeddings with the *da* complementizer but not in embeddings with the infinitival complementizer thus squares with our hypothesis, according to which the embedded subject has been deleted in the latter case but not in the former.

Some additional support for this analysis comes from the so-called "impersonal construction" (*bezlična konstrukcija*) of Serbo-Croatian. I will not justify the analysis of the impersonal construction here, but the essential point is that sentences in the impersonal construction have a [+Pro, +Human] subject in deep structure which I will refer to simply as "Pro"; by this is meant not any pronoun, but rather the same entity that appears in surface structure as *on* in French and as *man* in German. In Serbo-Croatian, the underlying Pro subject is deleted in the course of the derivation, and the morpheme *se* is inserted into structures from which this underlying subject has been deleted.[11] This "impersonal *se*" acts as a clitic pronoun in surface structure. As a result, a deep structure like

(16)

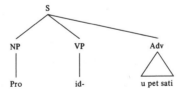

ends up as the sentence

(17) Ide se u pet sati.
go *se* at five o'clock
'Pro is going at five o'clock; on va à cinq heures.'

---

11 This is not meant to be a complete or even necessarily an accurate account of what happens in the course of the derivation. For example, it does not explain why it is that in Serbo-Croatian, as in many other languages, we find the reflexive morpheme in "impersonal" constructions of this sort. A better analysis would do this. It is also likely that the deletion of the underlying Pro subject is accomplished not by a special rule, but by the rule which deletes all nonemphatic subject pronouns in Serbo-Croatian.

If this sentence is embedded beneath a sentence in which *ja* 'I' is the subject of *želje-* 'want', we get the sentence

(18)   Želim da se ide u pet sati.
'I want that Pro go at five o'clock; je veux qu'on aille à cinq heures.'

The essential point is that sentences with the [+Pro, +Human] subject end up with the morpheme *se* in surface structure.

Now, the underlying Pro subject of the impersonal construction, like any other subject noun phrase, is subject to the application of Equi-NP Deletion if it is identical to the subject of the matrix sentence. Hence, if we have a deep structure like

(19)

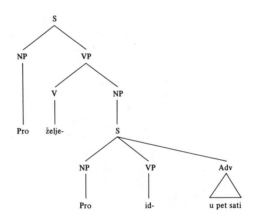

Equi-NP Deletion should be able to apply optionally. If our hypothesis is correct, the deletion of the subject of the embedded sentence should cause the appearance of the infinitival complementizer. Without application of Equi-NP Deletion we will get the *da* complementizer. Now, we have seen that the underlying Pro subject ends up as the morpheme *se*. Therefore, the number of *se*'s in the final string should correspond to the number of instances of this Pro subject. If the infinitive arises as a result of the deletion of the embedded subject, only one *se* should be possible with the infinitival complementizer. This is indeed the case.

(20)   Želi se ići.
'Pro wants to go; on veut aller.'

(21)   *Želi se ići se.

If the embedded subject has not been deleted, we should have two instances of the Pro subject, hence two instances of *se* in the surface structure. This too is the case.

(22)   Želi se da se ide.
'Pro wants to go; on veut aller.'

(20) and (22) are synonymous, as are (10a) and (11a). The fact that we get two *se*'s with the *da* complementizer but only one with the infinitival complementizer supports our hypothesis that the infinitive arises as a result of the removal of the subject of the embedded sentence.

Having established that the infinitival complementizer results from the deletion of the subject of the embedded sentence, we are now in a position to consider the evidence that certain verbs in Serbo-Croatian manifest a *deep structure constraint* to the effect that the subject of a sentence embedded beneath them must be identical to their own subject. We will see that Lakoff's notion of "absolute exception" to the rule of Equi-NP Deletion, requiring both that the structural description of Equi-NP Deletion be met and that the rule actually apply, cannot adequately account for the facts in Serbo-Croatian.

The verb *namjeravati* 'intend' exhibits the properties in question. We find sentences like

> **(23)** Namjeravam da idem.
> 'I intend that I go; I intend to go.'

with the *da* complementizer and inflection of the verb *idem* to agree with its first person singular underlying subject *ja*. In addition, there are grammatical sentences with the infinitival complementizer like

> **(24)** Namjeravam ići.
> 'I intend to go.'

in which Equi-NP Deletion has deleted the subject of the embedded sentence, resulting in an infinitive. (23) and (24) are analogous to (10a) and (11a). What makes *namjeravati* different from *željeti* is the fact that whereas (10b) and (10c) with *željeti* are grammatical, the corresponding sentences with *namjeravati* are not.

> **(25)** a. *Namjeravam da ideš.
> 'I intend that you go.'
> b. *Namjeravam da Rastko ide.
> 'I intend that Rastko go.'

Sentences with *namjeravati* are grammatical just in case the subject of the embedded sentence is identical to the subject of *namjeravati*. The paradigm with a second person singular subject is therefore:

> **(26)** a. *Namjeravaš da idem.
> 'You intend that I go.'
> b. Namjeravaš da ideš.
> 'You intend to go.'
> c. *Namjeravaš da Rastko ide.
> 'You intend that Rastko go.'

It is clear that the formalism of "absolute exceptions to Equi-NP Deletion" cannot account for these facts. To use this formalism, we would have to require that the structural description of Equi-NP Deletion be met and that the rule actually apply. But in (23) and (26b) Equi-NP Deletion has not applied. If it had, an infinitive would have resulted. The constraint on the subject embedded beneath verbs like *namjeravati,* then, is not statable as a constraint on the Equi-NP Deletion transformation.

It is now reasonable to ask whether it might be possible to devise some other way of stating this constraint as a transformational constraint. Two ways of doing this suggest themselves, and we shall examine them in turn.

The first way that comes to mind of stating the like-subject constraint in Serbo-Croatian by means of tranformations would be to require that the structural description of the Equi-NP Deletion transformation be met, even though the rule need not actually apply. To do this would require a change in the theory of grammar, but it would be able to account for the facts of (23), (25), and (26). While this seems a highly dubious maneuver, rather than discuss its undesirability I will simply point out that there are other facts in Serbo-Croatian which it cannot handle. The Equi-NP Deletion transformation in Serbo-Croatian must be constrained so that the subject of the embedded sentence will be deleted only if it is identical to the *subject* of the higher sentence; it is never deleted upon identity to the *object* of the higher sentence.[12] As a result, Equi-NP Deletion does not apply with verbs like *prisiliti* 'force' and other verbs which occur in the type of structure that Rosenbaum calls "transitive verb phrase complementation." But the verbs which occur in these structures require that the subject of the embedded sentence be identical to the *object* of the matrix sentence. With a first person singular object in the matrix sentence, then, we find

> **(27)** a. Prisilio me je da idem.
> 'He forced me that I go; he forced me to go.'
> b. *Prisilio me je da ideš.
> 'He forced me that you go.'
> c. *Prisilio me je da ide.
> 'He forced me that he go.'

while with a second person singular object in the matrix sentence we find

> **(28)** a. *Prisilio te je da idem.
> 'He forced you that I go.'
> b. Prisilio te je da ideš.
> 'He forced you that you go; he forced you to go.'
> c. *Prisilio te je da ide.
> 'He forced you that he go.'

In each case the subject of the embedded sentence must be identical to the *object* of the matrix sentence. But there is no possibility of stating this constraint by requiring that the structural description of Equi-NP Deletion be met, for the structural description must specifically be constrained so as to exclude its application to these structures in order to avoid converting the structures underlying (27a) and (28b) into the ungrammatical

---

12 See note 8.

(29)   *Prisilio me je ići.
           'He forced me to go.'

and

(30)   *Prisilio te je ići.
           'He forced you to go.'

respectively. Hence it simply will not do to require that the structural description of Equi-NP Deletion be met.

A second possibility might be to look for some other transformation in terms of which to state the like-subject constraint as a transformational constraint. Such an attempt would be misguided, however, because in the case of verbs like *namjeravati* 'intend', the constraint holds between the subjects of two (vertically) adjacent sentences and Equi-NP Deletion is the only transformation that states an identity constraint between these two noun phrases. In the case of verbs like *prisiliti* 'force', moreover, the constraint holds of a pair of noun phrases which is not looked at by any transformation in the grammar.

For these reasons, we cannot use the transformations of Serbo-Croatian to reject as ungrammatical any sentence in which the subject of a sentence embedded beneath *namjeravati* is not identical to the subject of *namjeravati,* or a sentence in which the subject of a sentence embedded beneath *prisiliti* is not identical to the object of *prisiliti.* We need *deep structure constraints* to do this. As was pointed out in connection with the unlike-subject constraint in English, these constraints differ from transformations not only in that they effect no change in phrase markers, but also in that their "structural description" must be met if a grammatical sentence is to result. They are therefore different from obligatory transformations, which apply *if* their structural description is met. Furthermore, if they were transformations they could be ordered with respect to other transformations. This would give us an exceedingly powerful device. It seems that we can constrain these filtering devices and claim that they apply only to the input to the transformational component.

2 SURFACE STRUCTURE CONSTRAINTS IN SYNTAX

0. INTRODUCTION

Standard grammars of Spanish point out that the weak or atonic forms of the object pronouns must come in a certain fixed order. For example, both Gili y Gaya (1961, 237) and the Royal Spanish Academy (1931, 202) state that when there is more than one object pronoun, the second person pronoun always precedes the first person, and either of these pronouns precedes the third person pronoun, and that the clitic pronoun *se* must precede them all. Stockwell, Bowen, and Martin (1965, 194) give a chart which is essentially equivalent to this statement.

It is the purpose of this chapter to explore the implications of this well-known fact for linguistic theory.

In the theory of syntax of Chomsky (1965), deep structures which have been generated by phrase structure rules and into which lexical items have been inserted are mapped onto surface structures by grammatical transformations. The transformations perform a "filtering function" in that the failure of an obligatory transformation to apply causes a derivation to block; such sentences are thereby characterized as ill formed. To quote Chomsky:

> Not all generalized Phrase-markers generated by the base will underlie actual sentences and thus qualify as deep structures. What, then, is the test that determines whether a generalized Phrase-marker is the deep structure of some sentence? The answer is very simple. The transformational rules provide exactly such a test, and there is, in general, no simpler test. A generalized Phrase-marker M_D is the deep structure underlying the sentence S, with the surface structure M_S, just in case the transformational rules generate M_S from M_D.

Reprinted from *Linguistic Inquiry*, Vol. 1, No. 2, April 1970.

The surface structure M_S of S is well-formed just in case S contains no symbols indicating the blocking of obligatory transformations. A deep structure is a generalized Phrase-marker underlying some well-formed surface structure. Thus the basic notion defined by transformational grammar is: *deep structure M_D underlies well-formed surface structure M_S.* The notion "deep structure" itself is derivative from this. The transformational rules act as a "filter" that permits only certain generalized Phrase-markers to qualify as deep structures.[1]

In this chapter, evidence is presented to show that in Spanish there are ungrammatical sentences which cannot be characterized as such in a natural way by the blocking of obligatory transformations in the manner described above. It is necessary to strengthen grammatical theory by the addition of *surface structure constraints* or *output conditions* that the output of the transformational component must satisfy.[2] In particular, it is shown that the fixed order of object pronouns in Spanish is determined by such a surface structure constraint. This constraint is to be interpreted as a template or filter that is applied to sentences generated by the transformational component. If the object pronouns in sentences generated by the transformations are in the correct order, the sentence is grammatical. If not, it is discarded as ungrammatical. It is shown that as a result of the surface structure constraint on object pronouns in Spanish, there are well-formed deep structures to which there correspond no grammatical surface structures.

Throughout the chapter, the terms "surface structure constraint" and "output condition" are used interchangeably. Both terms seem appropriate, since I know of no compelling evidence that transformations can apply subsequent to the application of a surface structure constraint. On the other hand, there is also no evidence that there could not be any such transformations in any language. The quesion of whether or not "surface structure constraints" or "output conditions" apply only after the application of the last transformation is therefore left open here.

The argument proceeds as follows. In section 1, I will motivate the spurious *se* rule, which plays an important role in the argument that follows. In section 2, it is shown that certain sequences of Spanish object pronouns always result in ungrammatical sentences. In order to prevent sentences with such pronoun sequences from being generated transformationally, one would have to constrain more than one transformation to prevent each ungrammatical pronoun sequence from arising. In the case of one ungrammatical pronoun sequence—*se se*—it is shown that the kind of constraint one must impose is unstatable as a transformational constraint.

---

1 Chomsky (1965, 138–139).

2 The notion "output condition" and its inclusion in linguistic theory was first proposed within the theory of generative grammar by Ross (1967), Chapter 3. In an unpublished paper unknown to me when I was doing the work reported here, Langacker (1967) suggested that some kind of blocking device is needed in order to characterize as ungrammatical sentences with certain sequences of object pronouns in French.

It is concluded that one must state a well-formedness condition that the output of the transformational component must meet. Section 3 proposes a notation to incorporate significant generalizations in the statement of this constraint. It is proposed that this notation is universal and that constraints on the relative order of clitics are to be stated as surface structure constraints expressed in the proposed notation in all human languages. It is shown that the proposed universals predict what kinds of generalizations can emerge from data concerning clitics in other languages, and that generalizations of exactly the predicted type emerge from such data in French. In section 4, it is shown that the constraint on the relative order of clitic pronouns in Spanish can not be stated transformationally, nor can the effect of this constraint be put into the phrase structure rules which generate underlying structures. In section 5, some of the theoretical implications of this work are discussed.

1. THE SPURIOUS se RULE

In Spanish, object pronouns exist in both a "strong" and a "weak" or "clitic" form. I give here a list of the object pronouns which will appear in what follows.[3]

	Strong Form	Weak Form Dative	Weak Form Acc.
1st person singular	mí	me	me
2nd person singular	ti	te	te
3rd person sing. masc.	él	le	lo
3rd person sing. fem.	ella	le	la
1st person plural	nosotros	nos	nos
3rd person plural masc.	ellos	les	los
3rd person plural fem.	ellas	les	las
3rd person reflexive (sg. & pl.)	sí	se	se

---

[3] It will be observed that the masculine third person Accusative pronouns given here are *lo* and *los,* in conformity with Latin American usage, rather than the *le* and *les* that are used for human or animate objects in the Castilian dialect, for this paper presents data from a variety of Latin American Spanish. Even within Latin America, there seems to be a great deal of variation from one dialect to another with respect to the syntax of the object pronouns. The grammatical judgments presented here are those of informants from three geographically separated countries of Latin America—Costa Rica, Argentina, and Peru. Where some informants disagreed with particular judgments presented here, this fact is noted. No claim is made that the judgments of grammaticality presented here are representative of the speech of these regions, for in view of the great amount of dialectal variation, any such claim would be absurd. It is claimed only that there exists a variety of Latin American Spanish in which each of the arguments developed here is valid. It is certain that many speakers of Spanish will disagree with some of the judgments of grammaticality presented here. In each such case, the only interesting question is not whether the data is different in different dialects, but rather whether such data provides crucial evidence for an alternative theory to the one developed here.

Only in the third person are the reflexive and nonreflexive forms of the pronouns distinguished. A handful of forms which will not be relevant to our discussion have been omitted.

The strong form of the object pronouns appears under emphasis and in positions of contrast as in

(1) Elena no la vio a ella sino a él.[4]
'Elena saw not her but him.'

The strong form also appears after prepositions:

(2) Elena limpió la casa para él.
'Elena cleaned the house for him.'

We will not be concerned here with the distribution of strong as opposed to weak forms of the object pronouns, but only with the weak or clitic forms.

As can be seen in (1), the strong forms of object pronouns (e.g. *ella*) follow the verb. This is also the case with nonpronominal objects.

(3) Elena vio a Carmelina.
'Elena saw Carmelina.'

The clitic pronouns, however, cannot stand after a finite verb but must precede it.

(4) *Elena vio (a) la.

(5) Elena la vio.
'Elena saw her.'

The clitic *se* is the third person reflexive pronoun and has the strong form *sí*. However, a number of occurrences of *se* cannot be accounted for as weak forms of *sí*. We will now proceed to determine the origin of these instances of *se*.

In some sentences we have a choice between using the strong or weak form of a pronoun.[5]

(6) a. Lo recommendé a ti.
　　　b. Te lo recomendé.
　　　　'I recommended it to you.'

The weak form of the third person singular Dative pronoun is *le*. We find it, for example, in:

---

4 In some sentences, as in this one, the strong form of the pronoun (*ella*) is repeated in the weak or clitic form (*la*). The preposition *a* appears before certain nonclitic direct objects.

5 Some speakers do not like sentences like (6a), preferring (6b) or *Te lo recomendé a ti,* in which *a ti* has been repeated as the clitic pronoun *te*. Since essentially the same argument in support of the spurious *se* rule can be constructed for these dialects, this dialectal difference has no bearing on our argument and is ignored in what follows.

(7) Le recomendé ese hotel.
'I recommended that hotel to him.'

But in sentences analogous to (6) we find:

(8) a. Lo recomendé a él.
    b. *Le lo recomendé.
    c. Se lo recomendé.
    'I recommended it to him.'

Instead of the expected *le* we find *se*. This happens whenever we have two third person pronouns—a Dative and an Accusative—regardless of the number and gender of the pronouns. In other words, the following combinations of pronouns never occur:

(9)   *le lo   *le los   *le la   *le las
       *les lo   *les los   *les la   *les las

In each case we find, instead of *le* or *les,* the pronoun *se,* which, to distinguish it from the reflexive pronoun *se,* I will refer to as "spurious *se.*" I will follow traditional grammars of Spanish in claiming that spurious *se* arises through the following rule:

(10)   Spurious *se* rule: (obligatory)

$$\begin{bmatrix} \text{Pro} \\ \text{III} \\ \text{Dative} \end{bmatrix} \quad \begin{bmatrix} \text{Pro} \\ \text{III} \\ \text{Acc.} \end{bmatrix}$$
$$1 \qquad\qquad 2 \longrightarrow se, 2$$

where "III" simply means "third person."

This rule accounts for the fact that the pronoun sequences (9) do not occur, at the same time that it accounts for the appearance of spurious *se.* For what else could be the origin of this *se*?

Since *se* is the third person reflexive pronoun, we might be tempted to think that the *se* in (8c) is also a reflexive pronoun. But reflexive *se* can occur only if the subject is third person.[6] That is, we find paradigms like the following, in which the (a) sentences have a first person subject, the (b) sentences have a second person subject, and the (c) sentences have a third person subject.[7]

(11) a. *Se recomendé.
      se I recommended

---

[6] This may be an oversimplification, but the conditions on the occurrence of reflexive pronouns in complex sentences do not concern us here.

[7] The subject does not actually appear in surface structure, because nonemphatic subject pronouns in Spanish are deleted late in derivations.

    b. *Se recomendaste.
      se you recommended
    c. Se recomendó.
      se he recommended
      'He recommended himself.'

But in sentences like (8c), *se* can occur with a first or second person subject, as well as with a third person subject.

(12) a. Se lo recomendé.
       se it I recommended
       'I recommended it to him.'
      b. Se lo recomendaste.
       se it you recommended
       'You recommended it to him.'
      c. Se lo recomendó.
       se it he recommended
       'He recommended it to him.' [8]

The *se* in (12) has an entirely different distribution from the reflexive *se* in (11). Furthermore, the occurrence of *se* in (12) depends on the presence of a third person Accusative pronoun—in this case *lo*. If *recomendar* has a full noun phrase object instead of *lo*, we cannot use *se* here. For example, corresponding to (12a) there is no sentence

(13) *Se recomendé   ese hotel.
      se I recommended that hotel

Finally, genuinely reflexive instances of *se* can occur in the strong form *sí* accompanied by *mismo*. Corresponding to (11c) we find

(14) Se recomendó   a sí mismo.
      'He recommended *himself*.'

But there is no grammatical sentence with the reflexive strong form *sí* which would correspond to (8c/12a):

(15) *Se lo recomendé a sí mismo.

We must conclude that the *se* in (8c) and (12) is not a reflexive pronoun.

    There is further syntactic evidence that spurious *se* originates from a third person Dative pronoun, as the rule (10) would have it. We can see this in sentences in which the clitic pronouns are used redundantly—that is, we find a clitic pronoun *in addition to* a nonpronominal noun phrase or strong form pronoun. In such cases the clitic pronoun must be the same person, number, and case as the full noun phrase of which it is a pronominal copy. In sentences with "Dislocation," in which a noun phrase has been

---

8 The phrase translated as 'to him' in these examples could also be 'to her' or 'to them'. Similarly, the subject of (11c) and (12c) could also be feminine.

preposed, the sentence must obligatorily contain a pronominal copy of the dislocated noun phrase.[9]

(16) a. Luis comió el pan.
        b. *El pan Luis comió.
        c. El pan Luis lo comió.
           'Luis ate the bread.'

Here the direct object has been dislocated, and we consequently have the Accusative pronoun *lo* obligatorily reoccurring in the sentence. Under Dislocation of the indirect object we find a Dative pronoun reoccurring obligatorily.

(17) a. *A ella recomendé ese hotel.
        b. A ella le recomendé ese hotel.
           'I recommended that hotel to her.'

Now, if *ese hotel* has been pronominalized to *lo* we get:

(18) a. Lo recomendé a ella.
        b. *A ella lo recomendé.
        c. *A ella le lo recomendé.
        d. *A ella se lo recomendé.
           'I recommended it to her.'

It is clear that the redundant pronoun occasioned by Dislocation is *se*. Since the dislocated constituent is Dative (cf. (17b)) and third person, spurious *se* must be derived from a third person Dative pronoun.

Looking at it from the opposite direction, we see that when spurious *se* occurs, the dislocated noun phrase may be any third person noun phrase:

(19) A los bomberos que conocí en Nueva York se lo recomendé.
       'I recommended it to the firemen I met in New York.'

But it must be third person:

(20) a. *A ti se lo recomendaron.
        b. *A mí se lo recomendaron.
        c. *A nosotros se lo recomendaron.

All of these facts are automatically accounted for by the spurious *se* rule, which derives spurious *se* from a third person Dative pronoun.

If spurious *se* had any origin other than that proposed here, one would have to account for the strange fact that whereas in general the redundant pronoun is *obligatory* under Dislocation, in just these cases the redundant pronoun can not appear at all, and instead this strange *se* obligatorily *must* appear. But these otherwise strange facts are consequences of the spurious

---

[9] There are reportedly some dialects (e.g. in Ecuador) in which Dislocation does not entail this reduplicated pronoun. This argument and others based on this feature of standard Spanish would therefore not hold for such dialects.

se rule, which is thus very heavily motivated. This is important because this rule will play a crucial role in our argument.

It now remains to justify the particular formulation of the spurious *se* rule given in (10). We have already seen that only third person pronouns become *se*, and that this happens only before other third person pronouns. We have also seen that spurious *se* arises from a Dative pronoun. There are no grammatical sentences in which spurious *se* originates from an Accusative or Nominative pronoun. Hence the specification "Dative" in the first term of (10). Since spurious *se* is always followed by an Accusative pronoun, we have included the specification "Accusative" in the second term of (10).[10]

2. UNGRAMMATICAL SEQUENCES OF CLITIC PRONOUNS IN SURFACE STRUCTURE

We can now begin to examine the evidence that a surface structure constraint must be imposed on the output of transformations to block certain ungrammatical sequences of clitic pronouns in Spanish. In section 2.1, I will show that sentences with the pronoun sequences *me te* and *nos te* always result in ungrammatical sentences. In section 2.2, the same thing will be shown for the sequence *le me*. Section 2.3 shows that a number of different constructions would give rise to the pronoun sequence *se se*, but this sequence never occurs in grammatical sentences.

2.1. *me te and *nos te

The verb *escapar* used with a reflexive pronoun means 'to escape'. If a nonreflexive Dative of Interest (Ethical Dative) is added, it means 'to escape from someone', the "someone" being the nonreflexive Dative of Interest. In this construction, the reflexive pronoun must come first.

(21)   a. Te escapaste.
          'You escaped.'
       b. Te le escapaste.
          'You escaped from him.'
       c. Te me escapaste.
          'You escaped from me.'
       d. Te nos escapaste.
          'You escaped from us.'

However, if the subject is first person, the nonreflexive Dative constituent cannot be *te*.[11]

---

10 The inclusion of this specification in the spurious *se* rule will be justified in section 3, when the status of sentences with the pronoun sequences *le le* and *les les* is discussed.

11 Recall that the subject does not actually show up in surface structure, since it is deleted by a late rule.

(22) a. Me escapé.
          'I escaped.'
      b. Me le escapé.
          'I escaped from him.'
      c. *Me te escapé.
          'I escaped from you.'

(23) a. Nos escapamos.
          'We escaped.'
      b. Nos le escapamos.
          'We escaped from him.'
      c. *Nos te escapamos.
          'We escaped from you.'

How is the grammar to characterize *(22c) and *(23c) as ungrammatical? It seems necessary to impose on Spanish grammar a constraint something like:

(24) A sentence with a second person Dative of Interest and a first person reflexive pronoun is ungrammatical.

Now consider an entirely different construction—direct and indirect objects with verbs like *recomendar* 'recommend'. Pronominal indirect objects of such verbs may generally appear in either the strong form or the weak form.

(25) a. Manuel quería recomendarte a mí.
      b. Manuel quería recomendárteme.[12]
          'Manuel wanted to recommend you to me.'

But in some cases the pronoun may occur only in the strong form; use of the weak form results in an ungrammatical sentence.

(26) a. Manuel quería recomendarme a ti.
          'Manuel wanted to recommend me to you.'
      b. *Manuel quería recomendármete.

Substituting the first person plural pronoun for the first person singular above yields analogous results.

---

12 Some informants did not accept (25b) and (27b). For such speakers the argument presented here is not valid in its present form. The point of this argument, however, is that there are grammatical sentences with *te me* and *te nos,* but none with *me te* or *nos te.* This crucial fact also holds for the speakers who did not accept (25b) and (27b). They accepted sentences like *Quieren arrebatárteme* ('They want to steal you away from me') and *Quieren arrebatártenos* ('They want to steal you away from us'), which are quite analogous to (25b) and (27b). But these informants rejected as ungrammatical *Quieren arrebatármete* and *Quieren arrebatárnoste,* for there are no grammatical sentences with the pronoun sequences *me te* and *nos te.* One is therefore led to suspect that their nonacceptance of (25b) and (27b) may be due to idiosyncratic properties of certain constructions, like those with *recomendar.* This matter is taken up in section 3.6.1.

(27)   a. Manuel quería recomendarte a nosotros.
      b. Manuel quería recomendártenos.
       'Manuel wanted to recommend you to us.'

(28)   a. Manuel quería recomendarnos a ti.
       'Manuel wanted to recommend us to you.'
      b. *Manuel quería recomendárnoste.

In order to rule out ungrammatical sentences like *(26b) and *(28b) it would be necessary to impose a constraint something like:

(29)   The weak form of indirect object pronouns may not be used if the indirect object is second person singular and the direct object is first person.[13]

Comparing the constraints (24) and (29), it is clear that *the effect of both is to rule out sentences in which the pronoun sequences* me te *and* nos te *result.* Furthermore, the constraints (24) and (29) have no other motivation. To have to state these constraints separately, then, is to miss the generalization that regardless of their grammatical function, the presence of the pronoun sequences *me te* and *nos te* in surface structure causes the ungrammaticality of *(22c), *(23c), *(26b), and *(28b). It is generalizations of this kind, which cannot be stated deep structurally or transformationally, but only on the *output* of transformations, that a proper theory of language must be able to state.

2.2. *le me

Continuing to investigate sequences of clitic pronouns, we find that while the sequence *me le* is fully grammatical, there are no grammatical sentences with the pronoun sequence *le me.*

In sentences with two nonreflexive instances of the Dative of Interest, there is no intrinsic reason why they should have to come in one order and not another. Yet we find only the order *me le*—never *le me.*

---

13 Any attempt to make (29) or a modification of it actually work would encounter serious difficulties, for there are grammatical sentences in which the second person singular indirect object and the first person direct object are both clitic pronouns.

   (i)   Me ocupaste porque te me habían recomendado.
        'You hired me because they had recommended me to you.'

The facts are the same in sentences like

   (ii) Te me presenté.
        'I introduced myself to you.'

The grammaticality of (i) is subject to the caveat discussed in footnote 12. Actually, the sentence *Te me habían recomendado* seems to be ambiguous, the interpretation varying with the context with which it is supplied. It can mean either 'They had recommended me to you' or 'They had recommended you to me'. Since (29) will be rejected in favor of a surface structure constraint on the order of object pronouns in Spanish, these facts will be left here without further comment.

(30) a. Mi chiquita está triste porque me le quitaran la muñeca.[14]
'My little girl is sad because they took her doll away (from her (on me)).'
b. *Mi chiquita está triste porque le me quitaron la muñeca.

(31) a. Me le complicaron la vida a mi hija.
'They complicated my daughter's life on me.'
b. *Le me complicaron la vida a mi hija.

(32) a. Se me le perdió el pasaporte al niño.
'My child's passport got lost on me.'
b. *Se le me perdió el pasaporte al niño.

We must somehow account for the fact that the sequence *le me* never appears in these constructions.

In the case of indirect objects of *recomendar*, we also observe that the sequence *le me* never occurs. The indirect object clitic pronoun *can* precede the direct object pronoun, as in:

(33) a. Lo ocupé porque lo habían recomendado a mí.
b. Lo ocupé porque me lo habían recomendado.
'I hired him because they had recommended him to me.'

Those informants who accepted the sequence *te me* in sentences with *recomendar* also accepted these sentences:

(34) a. Me ocupaste porque me habían recomendado a ti.
b. Me ocupaste porque te me habían recomendado.
'You hired me because they had recommended me to you.'

But when using the weak form of the pronoun results in the sequence *le me*, the sentence is ungrammatical.

(35) a. Me ocupó porque me habían recomendado a él.
'He hired me because they had recommended me to him.'
b. *Me ocupó porque le me habían recomendado.[15]

---

14 I am indebted to Guillermo Segreda for calling to my attention examples of this kind.

15 This is actually the weakest point in this argument. I have shown sentences with *recomendar* in which the indirect object clitic pronoun precedes the direct object clitic, but I have not shown that we would really expect a sentence like *(35b) to be grammatical. There are additional puzzling facts in connection with sentences like these. One concerns the fact that the pronoun sequence *me le* with *recomendar* is ungrammatical.

(i) *Me le recomendó.
'He recommended me to him.'
(ii) *Ramón quería recommendármele.
'Ramón wanted to recommend me to him.'

It is not clear why these sentences are ungrammatical. This question is discussed briefly in section 3.6.1. These facts show that the output constraint that I propose in this paper is unable to filter out *all* ungrammatical sentences involving the clitic pronouns in Spanish. Still, the major point that I am making here is true: the clitic sequence *me le* occurs

Here, then, where *me* is Accusative and *le* is Dative, the sequence *le me* is ungrammatical, just as it is in (30–32), where both *me* and *le* are Dative. We need to have some way of ruling out sentences with the pronoun sequence *le me*, regardless of their source.

2.3. *se se

That it is necessary to rule out certain surface sequences of clitic pronouns can be seen in a particularly striking way in the case of the pronoun sequence *se se*, which has a number of opportunities of arising in Spanish. Yet it never does. I will now show that in order to block this ungrammatical pronoun sequence by constraining transformations, it would be necessary to refer to the output sequence *se se* itself; no other constraints on the transformations will suffice to rule out *se se*. Since it is necessary to refer to the output sequence *se se* anyway, it is clear that constraining the transformations themselves is completely beside the point. It suffices to rule out the sequence *se se* in final output.

2.3.1. Impersonal se and Spurious se. In addition to reflexive *se* and spurious *se,* there is a third source of *se* in Spanish. This kind of *se* I will call "impersonal *se*," for it arises as the result of an underlying *Pro* subject which is like *on* in French and *man* in German.[16]

(36)   En México se trabaja mucho.
       'In Mexico *Pro* ('one') works a lot.'

(37)   Se me permitió dormir toda la mañana.
       '*Pro* allowed (*se permitió*) me to sleep all morning,' i.e., 'I was allowed to sleep all morning.'

Spanish sentences with an underlying *Pro* subject have impersonal *se* in surface structure. This impersonal *se* behaves like a clitic pronoun in every respect.

2.3.1.1. Impersonal se, Spurious se, and S-Pronominalization. Spanish also has a phenomenon which I will refer to as "S-Pronominalization"; an S which is identical to a previous S in the sentence is replaced by the pronoun *lo*. As a result of these two phenomena we find sentences like

(38)   A Sarita se le permitió dormir toda la mañana, pero a mí no se me lo ha permitido.
       'Sarita was allowed to sleep all morning, but I wasn't allowed to.'

---

in grammatical Spanish sentences (although not everywhere we might expect it), but there are no grammatical sentences with the pronoun sequence *le me*.

16 The term *"Pro,"* as I use it, refers not to any pronoun, but rather to the entity which is the underlying subject of sentences like (36) and (37). I use *Pro* in English translations of Spanish sentences as well, since there is no equivalent of *Pro* in English.

The *lo* here has replaced the sentence (*yo*) *dormir toda la mañana* (cf. (37) above).[17] Recall that the repetition of the dislocated NPs (*a Sarita* and *a mí*) in pronominal form (*le* and *me*, respectively) is obligatory.[18]

Now, to show that the pronoun sequence *se se* results in an ungrammatical sentence, let us try to reverse *Sarita* and *mí* in the deep structure of (38). We end up with an ungrammatical sentence.

(39) a. *A mí se me permitió dormir toda la mañana, pero a Sarita no se le lo ha permitido.
      b. *A mí se me permitió dormir toda la mañana, pero a Sarita no se se lo ha permitido.
         'I was allowed to sleep all morning, but Sarita wasn't allowed to.'

*(39a) is ungrammatical because the spurious *se* rule has not applied; we saw in section 2 that the sequence *le lo* is never grammatical. The spurious *se* rule has applied in *(39b) but the sentence is still ungrammatical—because it contains the pronoun sequence *se se*. Finally, there is no low-level rule which converts the ungrammatical *se se* to *se*, since the sentence

(40) *A mí se me permitió dormir toda la mañana, pero a Sarita no se lo ha permitido.
      'I was allowed to sleep all morning, but he didn't allow Sarita to.'

is not accepted. The second half of *(40) would be perfectly grammatical by itself, for example in

(41) Ramón me permitió dormir toda la mañana, pero a Sarita no se lo ha permitido.
      'Ramón allowed me to sleep all morning, but he didn't allow Sarita to.'

Since the indirect object must obligatorily be repeated in pronominal form, the *se lo* in the second half of *(40) and (41) is the result of *le lo*, due to application of the spurious *se* rule. This is fully grammatical in (41), since the subject is *Ramón*. But in *(40), where the underlying subject *Pro* must be spelled out with *se*, the second half of the sentence cannot be interpreted as having the subject *Pro*, since the one *se* present is "used up" in the role of spurious *se* derived from *le*. Thus the first half of *(40) has the subject *Pro,* while the second half, if it can be interpreted at all, is felt to contain

---

17 The repeated sentence (*yo*) *dormir toda la mañana* is not identical in all respects to the antecedent sentence (*Sarita*) *dormir toda la mañana,* for the subjects of the two sentences are different. However, the requirement of identity is still satisfied. This is an example of what Ross (1967b and 1969a) calls "sloppy identity."

18 The doubling of indirect objects of this type as clitic pronouns is obligatory, whether or not they have been dislocated. This fact is relevant, since it means that it will not be possible to produce a grammatical sentence from the structure underlying *(39) by attempting to block the preposing of the indirect object.

a deleted third person pronominal subject other than *Pro.* *(40), then, has exactly the same status as

(42)   *A Sarita se le permitió dormir toda la mañana, pero a mí no me lo ha permitido.
'Sarita was allowed to sleep all morning, but he didn't allow me to.'

The subject of the first half of the sentence is *Pro*, while the subject of the second half is a deleted non-*Pro* third person pronoun—hence 'he', 'she', or 'it' in English translation. This creates an imbalance which is the source of the nonacceptability of *(40) and *(42). While (38) is a fully grammatical sentence, if *Sarita* and *mí* are interchanged in its deep structure, a grammatical sentence cannot result.

A grammar of Spanish must somehow characterize sentences like *(39b) as ungrammatical. There are at least three possibilities:

(a)   Constrain optional transformations so that they do not apply and therefore do not produce sentences like *(39b).
(b)   Cause an obligatory transformation to block, thereby characterizing the resulting sentence as ungrammatical.
(c)   Adopt a surface structure constraint which discards as ungrammatical any sentence with the pronoun sequence *se se* in surface structure.

The only optional transformation involved in the production of *(39b) that could conceivably be constrained is S-Pronominalization. If S-Pronominalization were prevented from applying in the derivation of this sentence, the result would be:

(43)   A mí se me permitió dormir toda la mañana, pero a Sarita no se le ha permitido dormir toda la mañana.
'I was allowed to sleep all morning, but Sarita was not allowed to sleep all morning.'

While (43) is redundant, it is grammatical. So it is in principle possible to emerge with a grammatical sentence from the deep structure underlying *(39b), if S-Pronominalization is somehow prevented from applying.

Now, how is S-Pronominalization to be prevented from applying in the derivation of (43) so that *(39b) is not produced? The application of S-Pronominalization cannot be constrained in general, for it has applied in (38) and yielded a grammatical sentence. Since the difficulty in *(39b) seems to have been caused by the subsequent application of the spurious *se* rule, we might try to block S-Pronominalization in environments in which its application makes it possible for the spurious *se* rule to apply subsequently. However, it is useless even to consider such a constraint, for in (41) S-Pronominalization has applied, making it possible for the spurious *se* rule to apply subsequently, and a grammatical sentence has resulted. What causes the ungrammaticality of *(39b) is the fact that the spurious *se* rule has applied in a sentence in which there is already a *se* present, resulting in the surface sequence *se se*. To prevent S-Pronominalization from applying in just this situation, we would have to have some way of specifying, *at the point in derivations at which S-Pronominalization applies,* the class of sentences that are potentially ungrammatical as the result of the application of subsequent rules (both obligatory and optional) that produce some ungrammaticality as a result of the fact that S-Pronominalization had previously applied. This information is not available at the point at which S-Pronominalization applies. It is available only after all relevant transformations have applied. For the constraint that must be stated is not a constraint on the operation of a particular transformation such as S-Pronominalization, but a constraint on the interaction of the output of S-Pronominalization with the output of other transformations. In short, it is not a transformational constraint, but rather a constraint on the *output* of the transformational component. The information that would be needed to block S-Pronominalization is available only after both S-Pronominalization and the spurious *se* rule have applied, at which point S-Pronominalization cannot be prevented from having previously applied. It is clear, then, that we cannot prevent *(39b) from being generated by constraining the rule of S-Pronominalization.

The same kinds of arguments serve to show that we cannot characterize *(39b) as ungrammatical by causing an obligatory transformation to block. The only transformations that could be relevant here are the spurious *se* rule, the rule that doubles the indirect object by placing a pronominal copy of it before the verb, and the rule that spells out the underlying *Pro* subject as the morpheme *se*. Picking one of these rules and saying that the derivation blocks if it applies would be perfectly arbitrary, and therefore unjustified. Furthermore, whichever of these rules we pick, we will encounter the same kind of difficulty we found in trying to constrain the rule of S-Pronominalization. If we try to make the spurious *se* rule block,[19] for

---

[19] The question should be raised of whether linguistic theory should allow *any* transformation to cause derivations to block. A low-level rule like the spurious *se* rule hardly seems like the kind of rule that should cause an entire derivation to block. Another point should also be raised in this connection. The "filtering function of transformations" seems best motivated in those cases where a metaconstraint of some kind can account for the "blocking" of a particular transformation. The examples discussed in Chomsky (1965), where it is proposed to give transformations this filtering function, concern phrase markers with relative clause structure where there is no noun phrase in the relative clause that is identical to the antecedent in the matrix sentence. Chomsky proposes that the identity constraint that these structures fail to satisfy is but a special case of a more general principle, which requires that deletion not take place unless the deleted constituent is recoverable in a sense that is made precise elsewhere in the book. Ross (1967b) shows many cases in which metaconstraints on transformations make it impossible to move a constituent out of a certain kind of structure. In cases where the movement rule is obligatory, the rule blocks and the sentence is thereby characterized as ungrammatical. In both Chomsky's and Ross's examples, some metacondition on transformations prevents a particular rule from applying, thereby characterizing the resulting sentence as ungrammatical. The question should therefore be raised as to

example, the conditions under which it blocks will have to be specified roughly like this: the spurious *se* rule blocks a derivation if it results in the presence of the pronoun sequence *se se* in surface structure. This is not a constraint on a transformation, but a constraint on a resulting surface structure.

We must conclude that constraining an optional transformation or causing an obligatory transformation to block is not the proper way to characterize the ungrammaticality of sentences like *(39b). Rather than constraining or blocking transformations, we will let them apply freely in sentences like *(39). We will then impose a surface structure constraint that discards sentences with the pronoun sequence *se se* as ungrammatical.

I will now proceed to show that the pronoun sequence *se se* in surface structure always results in ungrammaticality, regardless of how it arose.

2.3.1.2. Impersonal se, Spurious se, and Accusative Pronouns. In the sentence

(44) Se les da los honores a los generales.
  '*Pro* gives the honors to the generals,' i.e., 'The honors are given to the generals.'

the repetition of the indirect object as *les* is obligatory.[20] In sentences like this, if *los honores* is pronominalized to *los,* no matter what the reason for the pronominalization, an ungrammatical sentence will result. Thus we may say

(45) A los generales se les da los honores, pero a los conscriptos no se les da los honores.
  'To the generals the honors are given, but to the conscripts the honors are not given.'

but we may not follow the more natural course and pronominalize *los honores.*

(46) a. *A los generales se les da los honores, pero a los conscriptos no se les los da.
  b. *A los generales se les da los honores, pero a los conscriptos no se se los da.

---

whether *all* cases of the "filtering function of transformations" should not involve the blocking of particular transformations by metaconstraints of one kind or another. That is, linguistic theory should not allow us to impose *ad hoc* constraints on particular transformations which cause them to "block" in particular instances, such as would be necessary to characterize the sentences under discussion here as ungrammatical by the blocking of some transformation in their derivational history. These issues are taken up in the Epilogue.

20 Malcah Yaeger has informed me that in certain coastal dialects of South America, the doubling of the indirect object as a clitic pronoun is optional rather than obligatory. Arguments based on the obligatoriness of this doubling would therefore not hold for these dialects.

In *(46a) the spurious *se* rule has not been applied, while in *(46b) the pronoun sequence *se se* has resulted. Similarly, if we try to dislocate *los honores* in (44), thereby necessitating a repetition of *los honores* as the clitic pronoun *los,* it is impossible to obtain a grammatical sentence.

(47) a. *Los honores se les los da a los generales.
  b. *Los honores se se los da a los generales.

To see that this ungrammaticality is due to the resultant *se se* sequence, consider the sentence which is identical to (44) except that its subject is *el gobierno* 'the government' instead of *Pro*. This sentence has no impersonal *se*:

(48) El gobierno les da los honores a los generales.
  'The government gives the honors to the generals.'

Now it is possible to dislocate *los honores*:

(49) Los honores el gobierno se los da a los generales.[21]

since with no impersonal *se* present, the creation of spurious *se* does not lead to the ungrammatical pronoun sequence *se se*.

2.3.2. Impersonal se and Reflexivum tantum. There are other sentences in which the pronoun sequence *se se* should arise, but they, too, are ungrammatical. For example, consider verbs which must occur with a reflexive pronoun, somewhat like *perjure* in English. One such verb is *arrepentirse* 'repent'.

(50) a. *Cuando Sarita roba, arrepiente muy pronto.
  b. Cuando Sarita roba, se arrepiente muy pronto.
    'When Sarita steals, she repents very quickly.'

*(50a) is ungrammatical because it lacks the reflexive pronoun *se*. Now, suppose that the underlying subject of (50b) is not *Sarita* but rather *Pro*. *Pro* must be spelled out with impersonal *se*. For this reason no grammatical sentence can result.

(51) a. *Cuando se roba, se arrepiente muy pronto.
  b. *Cuando se roba, se se arrepiente muy pronto.
    'When *Pro* steals, *Pro* repents very quickly.'

*(51a) is ungrammatical because it does not have both the impersonal *se* that it needs to agree with the first clause, and the *se* required by *arrepentirse*.[22] *(51b) is ungrammatical because it contains *se se*.

---

21 Speakers of Spanish perturbed by the presence of both *los honores* and *el gobierno* at the beginning of (49) prefer *Los honores se los da a los generales el gobierno*. This difference in the position of the subject has no bearing on our argument.

22 Malcah Yaeger has told me that in certain coastal dialects of South America sentences like *(51a) are grammatical. Speakers of these dialects reportedly also find sentences like *(40) and *(62a) grammatical. This suggests that these dialects have a late, low-

If we attempt to characterize *(51b) as ungrammatical by causing some obligatory transformation in its derivational history to "block," we will have to arbitrarily pick one transformation and impose an *ad hoc* constraint on it to the effect that it "blocks" under just those conditions which would lead to the occurrence of the pronoun sequence *se se* in surface structure. Since the conditions which lead to ungrammaticality are a property of the resulting surface structure, to attempt to characterize the ungrammaticality as a transformational violation is to miss the point. Since a surface structure constraint to rule out as ungrammatical any sentence with *se se* in surface structure is needed anyway, independently of *(51b), it is clear that the same constraint should be used to characterize *(51b) as ungrammatical. *(51b) is, then, an example of a sentence with a well-formed deep structure to which there corresponds no well-formed surface structure. Cases of this kind constitute strong evidence for surface structure constraints.

In this connection, we should note that although there are grammatical sentences that at first may seem extremely close to *(51b) in meaning, they are not, in fact, paraphrases of it and therefore could not have the same underlying structure. Instead of *(51b) one might say:

(52)   Cuando uno roba, (uno) se arrepiente muy pronto.
'When one steals, one repents very quickly.'

using *uno* 'one' instead of *Pro* as the subject. In order to conclude that *(51b) is a sentence which has a well-formed deep structure but no corresponding grammatical surface structure, then, it is first necessary to establish that *uno* is not the same as the underlying *Pro* subject of sentences with impersonal *se*.

Both *uno* and the impersonal *se* construction have an underlying human

---

level rule which converts *se se* into *se*. The sentences generated by the transformational component in these dialects therefore do not contain the clitic sequence *se se,* and the result is grammatical. The existence of dialects of this sort raises the interesting question of whether the existence of surface structure constraints may not be responsible for certain earlier rules in the syntactic component. One might say that the reason these dialects have the rule which converts *se se* into *se* is to enable a number of sentences that would otherwise be unsayable to become grammatical. Of course, it would be incorrect to maintain that the existence of a surface structure constraint that discards certain sentences as ungrammatical *requires* the inclusion in the grammar of earlier rules that enable the relevant sentences to emerge as grammatical, since many dialects have no such rule to convert *se se* into *se*. Furthermore, as will be seen later in this chapter, there are sentences with a well-formed underlying structure to which there corresponds no grammatical surface structure. Such examples show that there is no general requirement that all well-formed underlying structures must be able to emerge from the grammar as grammatical sentences.

One speaker of Spanish reports that for her *(51a) and *(62a) are grammatical, but *(40) is not. The ungrammaticality of *(40) shows that her grammar does not contain a rule which converts all occurrences of *se se* into *se*. It is possible that it contains such a rule which applies under more restricted circumstances, or that the second half of *(51a) and *(62a) in her dialect contain an underlying *uno* 'one' which undergoes deletion. The question will be left open here.

subject.[23] However, there is a difference in meaning between them. For example, compare

(53) En Vietnam se sufre mucho.
'In Vietnam *Pro* suffers a lot.'

and

(54) En Vietnam uno sufre mucho.
'In Vietnam *ya* suffer a lot.'

The English translations are only approximate. While both (53) and (54) are statements about suffering in Vietnam, (54) is a statement based on first-hand knowledge. This difference between *uno* and impersonal *se* can be brought out by constructing sentences in which such a report based on first-hand knowledge would be anomalous. If the verb is in the present progressive, it generally describes an action taking place at the time of the utterance. If *en Vietnam* is changed to *en esos países lejanos* 'in those distant countries', the action is reported as taking place in a place distant from the speaker. The resulting sentence with impersonal *se* is perfectly natural.

(55) En esos países lejanos se está sufriendo mucho.
'In those distant countries *Pro* is suffering a lot.'

But it is impossible to report what is taking place at the time of the utterance in a distant place *on the basis of first-hand knowledge*. Since (54) is a statement based on first-hand knowledge or experience, use of *uno* instead of impersonal *se* in (55) should result in an anomalous sentence. And it does.

(56) *En esos países lejanos uno está sufriendo mucho.
'In those distant countries yer suffering a lot.'

The actual semantics of *uno* and impersonal *se*, of course, remain to be worked out, and it is not at all clear how such facts are to be incorporated in a grammar. But the contrast between (55) and *(56) serves to show that *uno* and impersonal *se* are not the same.

Another aspect of the involvement of the speaker in sentences with *uno* is the fact that the speaker can use *uno* to refer to himself in an indirect or covert way. In some dialects, this possibility of using *uno* in place of a first person noun phrase has an interesting syntactic consequence: a female speaker using *uno* in this way would use the feminine form *una* instead of *uno*. As a result, adjectives which agree with it have to be feminine.

---

[23] In this section on *uno* and impersonal *se*, I have drawn on the discussion and examples in Otero (1966). I am indebted to Ivonne Bordelois, James Harris, and Carlos Otero for discussion of the meaning differences brought out here. Responsibility for errors is of course mine alone.

(57)   Una está satisfecha consigo misma.
'Yours truly is satisfied with herself.'

In (57), *satisfecha* and *misma* have the feminine ending -*a,* in agreement with the subject *una.* Impersonal *se,* which cannot be used to refer to the speaker, never occasions feminine adjective agreement.

(58)   *Se está satisfecha consigo misma.

Again, it is not clear how the fact that *uno* can be used "in place of a first person noun phrase" is to be incorporated in the grammar of Spanish. What *is* clear is that *uno* has this property, while the subject underlying the impersonal *se* construction does not. It follows that they are not the same entity.

Another difference between *uno* and the underlying subject of the impersonal *se* construction is to be found in the fact that only the latter can be used in sentences which require a plural subject.

(59)   A las cinco se empezó a llegar.
'At five o'clock *Pro* began to arrive.'

(60)   *A las cinco uno empezó a llegar.
'At five o'clock "one" began to arrive.'

Again, it is necessary to conclude that *uno* and impersonal *se* are different.

Evidence has been given to show that *uno* and the underlying subject of the impersonal *se* construction are not the same thing. Although (52) may at first seem to have the same meaning as *(51b), the two sentences can not have the same underlying structure. The fact remains that the deep structure underlying *(51b) is well formed but corresponds to no grammatical surface structure. A surface structure constraint is therefore necessary to discard *(51b) as ungrammatical.

2.3.3. Impersonal se and Reflexive Dative. Another case where the pronoun sequence *se se* should arise is in sentences with an underlying *Pro* subject and a Dative of Interest identical to the subject, which will then reflexivize and become reflexive *se.* The resulting sentence, with both impersonal *se* and reflexive *se,* will be ungrammatical. Thus alongside

(61)   Cuando come, Manfredo se lava las manos antes.
'When he eats, Manfredo washes his hands beforehand.'

where the Dative of Interest shows up as reflexive *se,* we cannot have such a Dative of Interest with impersonal *se* deriving from an underlying *Pro* subject:

(62)   a.   *Cuando se come, se lava las manos antes.
b.   *Cuando se come, se se lava las manos antes.
'When *Pro* eats, *Pro* washes *Pro's* hands beforehand.'

While *(62a) might be grammatical with a reading in which *las manos* are not '*Pro's* hands' but rather some plastic hands kept on a shelf (i.e., alienable rather than inalienable possession), it is ungrammatical as a realization of a deep structure like (61), but with *Pro* rather than *Manfredo* as subject. This is because there is only one *se*, while this deep structure would yield two—reflexive *se* stemming from the Dative of Interest and impersonal *se*. *(62b), on the other hand, is a correct realization of the deep structure in question but is ungrammatical because it contains the pronoun sequence *se se*. It is like *(51b) in that here too a well-formed deep structure corresponds to no grammatical surface structure. Only a surface structure constraint can characterize such sentences as ungrammatical.

2.4. Summary

In section 2 it has been shown that certain sequences of clitic pronouns never appear in surface structure in grammatical sentences of Spanish. In section 2.1 it was seen that two separate transformational constraints would be needed to prevent the generation of sentences with the pronoun sequences *me te* and *nos te* in surface structure. Section 2.2 showed that although the clitic sequence *me le* is grammatical, *le me* never occurs in grammatical sentences. In section 2.3 evidence was presented to show that if the transformations of Spanish are allowed to operate on well-formed deep structures, a number of sentences with the clitic sequence *se se* will result. Yet no such sentences are grammatical. In section 2.3.1 it was shown that when an Accusative pronoun turns up in a sentence which already contains impersonal *se* and a third person Dative pronoun, it triggers the spurious *se* rule; the resulting sentence contains the pronoun sequence *se se* and is ungrammatical. In section 2.3.1.1 it was seen that S-Pronominalization can not be constrained within present theory so as to prevent this from happening. In section 2.3.2 it was shown that in sentences with both impersonal *se* and a *reflexivum tantum,* the *se se* sequence which results causes the sentence to be ungrammatical. As a result, there are sentences which have a well-formed deep structure, but no corresponding well-formed surface structure. In section 2.3.3 it was shown that the *se se* sequence resulting from impersonal *se* and a reflexive third person Dative pronoun also causes the sentence to be ungrammatical.

There is abundant evidence, then, that the pronoun sequences *me te, nos te, le me,* and *se se,* regardless of their origin, result in ungrammatical sentences. The grammar of Spanish must contain a device to filter out any sentence which contains one of these pronoun sequences in surface structure.

3. DEVELOPING A NOTATION TO STATE THE CONSTRAINT

It has been shown that a number of sequences of pronouns in surface structure always result in ungrammatical sentences, no matter which transformations have applied to produce them. The grammar of Spanish must therefore include a surface structure constraint to rule out certain outputs of the transformational component. We will state this constraint for Spanish. Then we will attempt to extract what is universal and state it once and for all in linguistic theory, so that linguistic theory will make correct predictions about surface structure constraints on clitics, both in Spanish and in other languages.

3.1. Notation as a Means of Expressing Generalizations

The most direct way to state the constraint would be simply to list the ungrammatical sequences of pronouns. The constraint could then be stated as follows:

> **(63)** If the output of the transformational component contains any of the following sequences of pronouns, the sentence is ungrammatical:
>
> me te
> nos te
> le me
> se se

This would be adequate for the data already considered. But this method of ruling out ungrammatical pronoun sequences makes no predictions whatsoever about the grammaticality of further, as yet not considered, possible sequences of pronouns. It would certainly be preferable to state the constraint in such a way that it will predict speakers' intuitions about additional possible pronoun sequences.

We can begin by examining the ungrammatical pronoun sequences in (63) to see whether any generalizations emerge. Note first that both *me te* and *nos te* are ungrammatical. Since both *me* and *nos* are first person pronouns, both of these sequences can be excluded by means of a single statement:

> **(64)** If the output of the transformational component contains a first person pronoun followed by a second person pronoun, the sentence is ungrammatical.

Continuing in (63), note that *le* may not precede *me*. Seeking to generalize this constraint, we find that not only *le,* but also its plural, *les,* may not precede *me*. There are grammatical sentences like

> **(65)** Me les escapé.
> 'I escaped from them.'

but there are no grammatical sentences with the pronoun sequence *les me*. These facts extend to the first person plural clitic *nos,* which may precede *le* and *les* but can not follow them. The constraint that rules out *le me* can now be given in a more general form:

> **(66)** If the output of the transformational component contains a third person Dative clitic pronoun followed by a first person clitic, the sentence is ungrammatical.

As they are stated above, (64) and (66) are two totally unrelated constraints, which cannot be collapsed or combined into a single constraint. The notation (or lack thereof) in (64) and (66) therefore claims that there is no generalization which unites them. We must now face the question of whether there is, in fact, some generalization from which both (64) and (66) follow as special cases.

(64) and (66) state that certain pronoun sequences are ungrammatical. To impose such a constraint, then, is essentially to pass some kind of a template or filter over sentences generated by the transformational component—a template which characterizes the ungrammatical pronoun sequences—and to discard sentences which conform to this template. This filtering nature of the output constraint can be made explicit by stating directly the sequences of clitics that are ungrammatical, restating (64) as follows:

(67)   Output condition on clitic pronouns: *I   II

This has the same meaning as (64): any sentence with a first person clitic pronoun followed by a second person clitic pronoun must be discarded as ungrammatical. Similarly, (66) can be given as:

(68)   Output condition on clitic pronouns: *III   I
                                                 Dat

(67) and (68) are notational variants of (64) and (66), but they make explicit the fact that we are using the condition as a filtering template, discarding anything that conforms to it. And now that (64) and (66) have been rewritten as (67) and (68), it is possible to formulate a more general constraint from which the two constraints follow as special cases. (67) and (68) mean that if a sentence contains two clitic pronouns in the order given, the sentence is ungrammatical. Using exactly the same interpretation of the notation of (67) and (68), they can be combined into a single constraint:

(69)   Output condition on clitic pronouns: *III   I   II
                                                 Dat

(69) states a generalization from which (67) and (68) follow as special cases. Any putative generalization is an empirical claim, and it is therefore incumbent upon us to test this claim and to provide some evidence that the generalization expressed by (69) is a genuine generalization rather than an accidental or spurious one. This can be done once we note that (69) can be interpreted in such a way that it makes additional predictions which (67) and (68) do not make. (69) can be interpreted to mean that there will be no grammatical sentences of Spanish with the pronoun sequence: III II. This prediction is correct; there are no such grammatical
         Dat
sentences. Under the same interpretation, (69) does not rule out the sequence II III. And this sequence is grammatical.
        Dat

(70)   a. Te le escapaste.
               'You escaped from him.'

   b. Te les escapaste.
   'You escaped from them.'

The correctness of the additional predictions made by (69) with this interpretation constitutes empirical evidence that the generalization it expresses is a genuine one. It therefore supports the notation of (69) and the interpretation given to it, for only when the filtering function of the output constraint was made explicit by expressing (64) and (66) as (67) and (68) did it become possible to state the generalization from which the two constraints follow as special cases.

3.2. Positive versus Negative Notation

Now that the constraint is viewed as a template which filters out certain sentences generated by the transformational component, another question arises: should its statement be positive or negative? That is, instead of (69), which characterizes the *ungrammatical* pronoun sequences, should the output condition state instead the pronoun sequences that are *grammatical*? That is, we could adopt

(71)   Output condition on clitic pronouns: II   I   III
                                                          Dat

instead of (69). (71) is to be viewed as a template which characterizes the *grammatical* pronoun sequences, and any sentence containing a sequence of clitic pronouns that does *not* conform to (71) will be discarded as ungrammatical. The issue, then, is whether the output constraint is a template that characterizes ungrammatical pronoun sequences or grammatical ones. This again is an empirical question which must be decided one way or the other on the basis of empirical evidence.

In terms of the data considered so far, (69) and (71) are equivalent; the two proposed notations can be defined in such a way that they will accept and reject the same sequences of clitic pronouns. However, there is a crucial difference between the two notations. The positive notation of (71) will automatically rule out certain additional pronoun sequences which the negative notation of (69) is unable to rule out. If a given pronoun P is included in only one slot in the positive notation of (71), it will follow that sentences with the sequence P P will be ruled out as ungrammatical, since they will fail to conform to the filtering template. Thus, if the positive notation of (71) is adopted, it remains only to find the proper place in the chart for the clitic *se,* and it will follow *automatically* that sentences with the pronoun sequence *se se* will be discarded as ungrammatical. It has already been seen that *se se* sequences are ungrammatical, and that they cannot be blocked in a natural way by constraining the transformations. To block *se se* sequences with the negative notation of (69), it would be necessary to state an additional constraint such as

(72)   Sentences with the clitic sequence *se se* are ungrammatical.

or more generally, perhaps, as

(73) Sentences with two (or more) consecutive clitics having the same phonological shape are ungrammatical.

Since the positive notation of (71) will rule out sentences with *se se* automatically, we adopt this notation to state the surface constraint. In so doing, we are making the claim that the absence of *se se* sequences in Spanish is not an accident, but follows from the inclusion of *se* in only one column of a surface structure constraint expressed in this positive notation.

The claim that the notation of (71) "generalizes" to sentences with the clitic sequence *se se*, like any other such claim, is only as sound as the empirical evidence that supports it. It is not true *a priori* that sentences with *se se* should be filtered out by the same constraint that rules out sentences with other sequences of clitics. It might be argued that whereas certain other sequences of clitics are ruled out on syntactic grounds, *se se*— or any other sequence of two or more clitics with the same phonological shape—is ungrammatical for phonological reasons. To assert this position is to maintain that a constraint such as (72) or (73) is needed in the grammar independently of (69) or (71). However, there is some evidence that a constraint which filters out any sentence with two or more clitics of the same phonological shape is superfluous, and that what is needed instead is exactly what the positive notation of (71) provides—a constraint that discards as ungrammatical any sentence with two (or more) consecutive clitics *from the same slot of a constraint expressed in the notation of* (71).

We can base our argument on the fact that Spanish sentences with more than one Dative of Interest are grammatical.

(74) Ramón me le complicó la vida a mi hija.
'Ramón complicated my daughter's life on me.'

The clitic *me* is a first person singular Dative of Interest, while *le* is the obligatory clitic doubling of the Dative noun phrase *a mi hija*. Since sentences with two Datives of Interest are grammatical, there is nothing to prevent sentences with two third person Datives of Interest from being generated. The grammar will therefore produce sentences like

(75) a. *Ramón le le complicó la vida a su hija a mi amigo.
    b. *Ramón le le complicó la vida a mi amigo a su hija.
    'Ramón complicated my friend's daughter's life on him.'

But *(75) is ungrammatical. The spurious *se* rule does not apply to sentences like *(75), for if it did, *(76) would be grammatical.

(76) a. *Ramón se le complicó la vida a su hija a mi amigo.
    b. *Ramón se le complicó la vida a mi amigo a su hija.

This shows that the spurious *se* rule applies to *le* or *les* only if it is followed by a third person Accusative pronoun; this is the reason the specification 'Accusative' was included in the second term of the spurious *se* rule (10).

The fact that the spurious *se* rule does not apply to *(75) shows that some kind of filtering device is necessary to rule this sentence out.

The ungrammaticality of *(75) with its *le le* clitic sequence could be accounted for either by the positive notation of (71) or by a constraint like (73). The crucial sentences which decide between the two alternatives are those in which one of the third person Datives of Interest is singular and the other is plural. Such sentences are not grammatical either.

(77)   a. *Ramón le les complicó la vida a su hija a mis amigos.
           b. *Ramón les le complicó la vida a su hija a mis amigos.
           c. *Ramón le les complicó la vida a mis amigos a su hija.
           d. *Ramón les le complicó la vida a mis amigos a su hija.
              'Ramón complicated my friends' daughter's life on them.'

(78)   a. *Ramón le les complicó la vida a sus hijos a mi amigo.
           b. *Ramón les le complicó la vida a sus hijos a mi amigo.
           c. *Ramón le les complicó la vida a mi amigo a sus hijos.
           d. *Ramón les le complicó la vida a mi amigo a sus hijos.
              'Ramón complicated my friend's children's lives on him.'

Since the spurious *se* rule does not apply to sequences of two Dative pronouns, a filtering device is needed to discard *(77) and *(78) as ungrammatical.

A constraint like (73) cannot filter out *(77) and *(78) as ungrammatical. If the negative notation of (69) is adopted, we must abandon (72) and (73) and instead adopt the additional constraint:

(79)   Sentences with two (or more) clitics from the same slot of (69) are ungrammatical.

But if the positive notation of (71) is adopted, a constraint like (79) is completely superfluous, because it follows automatically from (71). The correct generalization is that ungrammaticality is caused not by sequences of two or more clitics of the same phonological shape, but rather by two or more clitics from the same slot in the surface constraint. The positive notation of (71) embodies exactly this generalization. We therefore adopt this notation, from which the ungrammaticality of *(75), *(77), *(78), and of sentences with the clitic sequence *se se* will follow as different instantiations of a single generalization.

3.3. Stating the Constraint for Spanish

It remains only to find the place of *se* in the output condition chart. Since there are sentences with the sequence *se te* such as

(80)   Se te perdió la llave.
        'The key got lost on you.'

se must precede II in the chart. The output constraint is therefore:

(81)   Output condition on clitic pronouns: *se*   II   I   III
Dat

(81) automatically characterizes as ungrammatical the sequence *se se*, as well as any of the following sequences, which consist of two clitics from the same slot of (81):

(82)   *te te
*me me
*nos nos
*me nos
*nos me
*le le
*les les
*le les
*les le

And this is correct; none of these pronoun sequences can occur.

With the notational convention that we have adopted, the constraint (81) does not rule out certain other clitic sequences. If there are no additional constraints which rule them out, the prediction is that the pronoun sequences *se me*, *se nos*, *se le*, and *se les* will be grammatical. This prediction is correct.

(83)   a.   Se me perdió la llave.
'The key got lost on me.'
b.   Se nos perdió la llave.
'The key got lost on us.'
c.   Se le perdió la llave.
'The key got lost on him.'
d.   Se les perdió la llave.
'The key got lost on them.'

At the same time, (81) predicts that no other clitic pronoun may precede *se*. This prediction is also correct; there are no grammatical sentences in which another clitic pronoun precedes *se*.

All the clitic pronouns have now been incorporated into the output constraint, except for the third person Accusative pronouns. They may follow first person pronouns:

(84)   a.   Miguel me lo recomendó.
'Miguel recommended it to me.'
b.   Miguel nos lo recomendó.
'Miguel recommended it to us.'

Given our notation, they must therefore follow "I" in (81). However, they may not precede the third person Dative pronouns. Sequences like *lo le*, *lo les*, *las le*, *las les*, and so on are ungrammatical. Since the third person Dative pronouns are converted to *se* before third person Accusative pronouns by the spurious *se* rule, it might at first seem necessary to put the third person Accusative pronouns after the third person Dative pronouns, yielding:

(85) Output condition on clitic pronouns: *se* II I III III

Dat Acc

Recalling that this condition must be used to discard as ungrammatical sentences with the sequence *se se* that arise as a result of the application of the spurious *se* rule, it is clear that this constraint must be applied at some stage in derivations *after* the application of the spurious *se* rule. This being the case, it is not necessary to allow third person Dative pronouns to precede third person Accusative pronouns in (81). The constraint can therefore be stated as follows: [24]

(86) Output condition on clitic pronouns: *se* II I III

The output condition (86) is again a test of the notation adopted to state this constraint. And (86) correctly predicts both that the pronoun sequences *te lo, te los, te la, te las, se lo, se los, se la,* and *se las* are grammatical and that the reverse sequences of pronouns—*lo te, los te,* and so on are ungrammatical. The correctness of these predictions furnishes empirical support for the notational conventions of (86).

3.4. Universals behind the Spanish Clitic Constraint

3.4.1. Universality of the Notation. The notation that has been used to state the output constraint on clitic pronouns in Spanish has consistently made correct predictions that go well beyond the data on which we based our statement of the constraint. Is this an accident? To state (86) in the grammar of Spanish and then leave matters there is to say that it is a property of the grammar of Spanish that does not follow from any properties of language in general. While it is conceivable that this is true, it is equally conceivable that (86) makes correct predictions about novel sentences in Spanish because it embodies something universal. It is necessary to discover what in (86) is universal, and to state it once and for all in linguistic theory, so that it need not be repeated in the grammars of Spanish and other languages. This task clearly cannot be completed here. We shall therefore content ourselves with making a tentative proposal about what in (86) is particular to Spanish and what is universal.

Let us begin by testing the strongest possible claim that could be made about the universality of (86):

(87) The constraint (86) is universal.

A theory which incorporates (87) says that in any language, clitics *must* come in the order *se II I III*. In such a theory, the constraint (86) will not need to be stated in the grammar of Spanish because it will be stated

---

[24] It is now no longer necessary that the spurious *se* rule be obligatory, since sentences in which it has failed to apply will be discarded as ungrammatical by the output constraint.

in universal grammar. This theory makes extremely strong claims; as far as clitics are concerned, it constrains the notion "human language" as severely as is possible, consistent with what we have already discovered about Spanish. For this reason, (87) is to be preferred to weaker theories, if it is correct. Unfortunately, however, (87) is incorrect. In French, for example, two third person clitic pronouns, a Dative and an Accusative, can co-occur in the same clitic group.

(88)   Marie *le lui* donnera.
       'Marie will give it to him.'

Since (87) would discard (88) as ungrammatical, (86) can not be part of the grammar of French and is therefore not universal. (87) must be abandoned. Our first attempt at extracting what is universal in (86) has been a failure, but that does not mean that we must give up. To do this would be to say that *everything* in (86) is accidental and language-particular, that *nothing* in (86) follows from general properties of human language. This might be so, but to take this position initially is to give up any hope of discovering whatever universal principles there may be that play a role in the constraint (86).

A more promising approach would be to postulate that it is the notation in which (86) is expressed that is universal, while the fact that (86) refers to the morpheme *se* and to the object pronouns by person, as well as the particular relative order in which they appear in (86), are particular to Spanish. I therefore tentatively propose that a proper linguistic theory will have to include (89).

(89)   Surface structure constraints on the relative order of clitics are to be stated in the template or chart notation of (86), with the interpretation it has been shown to have, in all natural languages.

It is not claimed that linguistic theory must necessarily include (89) in a list of linguistic universals. For example, (89) might follow automatically from some other principle. A theory in which it does is preferable to one in which it must be listed. It *is* claimed, however, that the content of (89) will have to be included in linguistic theory, whether as a separate statement or as an automatic consequence of some other principle.

Like the proposed universal (87), (89) must be tested empirically. If counterexamples show it to be too strong, it must be replaced by a weaker principle which will capture the maximal amount of (86) that is universal. It is also possible that (89) is not strong enough; it could turn out, for example, that there are universal principles governing the assignment of clitics to particular slots of (86) and the order of these slots relative to each other. In brief, (89) is an empirical hypothesis which must be tested against the facts of natural languages.

(89) is a very strong claim. It entails that in any language with a surface structure constraint on the relative order of clitics, the clitics are *strictly ordered*. That is, the relation "may precede," defined on slots of

charts like (86), is a transitive, antisymmetric, irreflexive relation. (89) entails that in all languages, constraints on relative clitic order are to be stated positively rather than negatively; the chart expresses the grammatical (rather than the ungrammatical) sequences of clitics, and sentences which do not conform to it are discarded. If universal grammar includes (89), it also follows that sentences containing more than one clitic from a given column of the output condition chart will be ungrammatical.

It would be well to emphasize that the interpretation given to the chart notation of (86) is not given *a priori,* but has been established on the basis of empirical evidence drawn from Spanish. For example, one can conceive of a linguistic theory which uses charts of the form (86) to state order constraints on clitics, but in which each slot A of the chart has the interpretation: an arbitrary string of A's. But if this interpretation is given to the slots of (86) in Spanish, it is not possible to account for the un-grammaticality of sentences with the clitic sequences *se se, le le, le les, les le,* and *les les.* We therefore interpret each slot to mean: one member only of the set assigned to this slot. (89) entails that in all languages the slots of charts in the notation of (86) will have this interpretation. This does not mean that in no language will we find grammatical clitic sequences of the form $A\ A$; a language that allowed this would simply have two slots allowing A. One can also conceive of a language with three slots allowing A; (89) predicts that in such a language, sequences of one, two, or three A's will be grammatical, but those of more than three will be ungrammat-ical. The essential point is that (89) entails that each slot will have the interpretation "one member only of the set assigned to this slot" in all languages. (89) therefore predicts that there will be languages in which only one member of a given set of clitics is allowed in a single clitic group. This prediction entails that a certain kind of generalization will emerge from linguistic data in languages not yet considered—namely, that we will find generalizations of the form: the clitics A, B, and C are mutually ex-clusive. Generalizations of this form will emerge because it is possible to assign more than one clitic to a given slot of a chart expressed in the nota-tion of (86), and each slot is universally interpreted as allowing only one member of the set assigned to that slot. One way to test the proposed universal (89), then, is to determine whether generalizations of this form do emerge from data on clitics in other languages.

One can also conceive of a linguistic theory that uses charts of the form (86) to express surface constraints on clitics, but that interprets these charts to mean that each slot *must* be filled or else the sentence is ungrammatical. Such a theory would not be able to account for the fact that in Spanish, sentences with sequences of fewer than four clitics are grammatical. (89) incorporates the claim that it is not an accident of Spanish, but rather a universal property of language, that charts like (86) mean that each slot may be filled *optionally.*

The proposed universal (89) also predicts which novel pairs of clitics will be grammatical, given a small number of grammatical pairs of clitics. For example, (86) could be set up on the basis of grammatical pairs of clitics of the form *se II, II I,* and *I III.* (86) has been interpreted to mean that the clitic pairs *III se, III II, III I, I se, I II,* and *II se* will be ungrammatical. As has been seen, these predictions are confirmed in Spanish. Now, one can conceive of a linguistic theory which uses the chart notation of (86) but which gives it a different interpretation. For example, (86) might have a "loop back" interpretation such that a clitic from the final slot of (86) could be followed by a clitic from the first slot. Given that the filling of each slot is interpreted to be optional, if the first slot is empty a clitic from the final slot could be followed by one from the second slot, or if that is empty by one from the third slot. Similarly, if the final slot is empty, a clitic from the penultimate slot could be followed by a clitic which precedes it in the chart, and so on. With this interpretation of (86), all possible pairs of clitics would be grammatical. There is no *a priori* reason why this should not be the case. The proposed universal (89), however, embodies the claim that this will not be the case in any language. It then follows from universal grammar that (86) does not have a "loop back" interpretation in Spanish.

3.4.2. Universality of Surface Structure Constraints on Clitics. In formulating the universal (89), we attempted to extract from the contraint (86) what is universal and should therefore not be stated repeatedly in the grammars of particular languages. We have put the *form* of the constraint (86) in universal grammar, while leaving the statement of which morphemes of Spanish are subject to the constraint in the grammar of Spanish. But is it an accidental and arbitrary fact of Spanish that it is the clitic pronouns that are subject to a surface structure constraint of the form (86) rather than, say, the strong forms of the pronouns, sentence adverbs, or prepositional phrases? To leave the matter here would be to miss the cross-linguistic generalization that in language after language, clitics are subject to the same kind of order constraint found in Spanish. I therefore tentatively propose that this is not an accidental property of particular languages, but rather follows from universal principles. The relevant generalization can be stated as follows:

(90)   In all languages in which clitics move to a particular place in the sentence, there are surface structure constraints on the relative order of clitics.[25]

---

[25] In languages in which the clitics do not move to the same place in the sentence, the question of their order relative to each other does not arise. This is the case in English, for example, where pronouns can be clitics which form a single phonological word with the word they attach to, but since the clitics are not all together in the same place there is no problem of specifying their relative order. (90) thus says that in a language like Spanish, in which the clitics move to the verb, they will be subject to a surface structure constraint. (89) states the notation in which the constraint must be stated. It seems that the position in the sentence to which clitics can move is also severely restricted by universal grammar: they can move to the verb, or to "second position" in the sentence. However, I will not go into these matters here.

One would want to construct a linguistic theory from which (90) would follow as an automatic consequence. Then we would have an explanation for (90) itself. However, it is not clear how this is to be done. For this reason, I simply state (90) for the present, so that its consequences can be tested. The intent of this proposal is that regardless of whether (90) needs to be stated as such in linguistic theory or follows automatically from something else, it is part of universal grammar. With (90) in universal grammar, the grammar of Spanish need not specify that it is the clitic pronouns that are subject to the surface structure constraint. Spanish grammar need specify only which elements are clitics in Spanish and the order in which they appear in (86). The rest is in Spanish because it is in universal grammar.

If (90) is correct, certain kinds of facts will appear in natural languages. A linguistic theory which includes (90) can therefore be said to provide an explanation of why facts of this kind are to be found in human languages. Several empirical consequences of (90) are sketched below.

A theory of language which did not include (90) would predict that clitics are likely to occur in the same order in deep structure and in surface structure, since their order in surface structure could be different only if there were special rules to rearrange them. But no such tendency is observable in natural languages. In French, for example, while case plays a role in the relative order of third person clitics, we find that there are some sentences in which the indirect object precedes the direct object

(91)   Gertrude *vous le* donnera.
       'Gertrude will give it to you.'

and others in which the direct object precedes the indirect object.[26]

(92)   Gertrude *le lui* donnera.
       'Gertrude will give it to him.'

In Spanish, where the object pronouns are arranged in surface structure by *person,* the underlying order of constituents plays no role whatsoever in determining the relative order of clitics in surface structure. Facts like this require an explanation. Why should surface structure order of clitics not mirror their underlying order, especially when this state of affairs requires adding additional rules to the grammar? The proposed universal (90) predicts that the order of clitics in surface structure will be determined solely by a surface structure constraint. It thus provides us with an explanation of why underlying and surface order of clitics are independent phenomena.

Second, since (90) requires that clitic order be determined by a surface structure constraint, it predicts that the only properties of clitic pronouns that can be relevant to their order are properties that are present in surface structure. If case, for example, is relevant to clitic order, and if there are transformations that change case in the course of the derivation

---

26 The behavior of clitic pronouns in French will be discussed in section 3.5.2.

so that the deep structure case and surface structure case of clitic pronouns are distinct, (90) predicts that only surface structure case can be relevant to clitic order. An example in which it is the underlying case of clitic pronouns rather than their case in surface structure that determines clitic order would constitute counterevidence to (90). (90) also raises the possibility that phonological properties of clitics may be relevant to their surface structure order. It remains to be seen whether or not examples of this exist in human languages.

There is one respect in which (90) makes a particularly strong claim. It asserts that in all languages the relative order of clitics will be fixed.[27] Whereas many languages have "free word order" in many respects, (90) predicts that no language will have "free clitic order." The existence of any such language would show (90) to be incorrect.

3.5. Testing Predictions Made by the Proposed Universals

(89) was established on the basis of data concerning *pairs* of clitics in Spanish. In section 3.5.1 it is shown that the predictions it makes about sequences of more than two clitics in Spanish are correct. In section 3.5.2 it is shown that (89) and (90), taken together, correctly predict the type of generalizations that will emerge from the data on clitics in French.

3.5.1. Sequences of More than Two Clitics in Spanish. Only *pairs* of clitics in Spanish have been considered so far. In the absence of a linguistic theory which makes specific predictions about sequences of more than two clitics, there is no reason to expect that any sequences of more than two clitics will be grammatical, or that some will be and others will not. The theory proposed here, however, makes quite specific predictions in this regard.

(86) has been interpreted to mean that a clitic from any slot in the chart may be absent, and that any two clitics must come in the order in which they are found in the chart. Since the presence of a clitic from any slot in the chart is optional, this interpretation of (86) entails that if there are no additional constraints on clitics, sequences of more than two clitics will also be grammatical. Furthermore, it automatically predicts that sequences of more than two clitics will be grammatical in Spanish if the clitics are in the order given in (86). If they are not, it predicts the sentence will be discarded as ungrammatical. A linguistic theory which includes (89) posits this interpretation of charts like (86) as universal. Such a theory is therefore a hypothesis concerning the ways data consisting of grammatical pairs of clitics will be generalized to sequences of more than two clitics in human languages. It thus provides an *explanation* of the grammaticality of sentences like (93–96).[28]

---

[27] This leaves open the possibility of clitic flip rules, which will be discussed briefly in footnote 35. Even if such rules exist, clitic order in a given environment is fixed.

[28] One speaker has informed me that in her dialect, no sentence with a sequence of more than two clitic pronouns can be considered fully grammatical. This dialect furnishes

(93)   *Se me le* perdió el pasaporte al niño.
'The (my) child's passport got lost on me.'

(94)   Nuestra hija, *te nos la* robaste.
'Our daughter, you stole her from us for yourself.'

(95)   *Te me le* echaste encima.[29]
'You threw yourself on him on me.'

(96)   Te le comiste el pan a Miguel, pero a mí no *te me lo* comas.
'You ate up Miguel's bread (on him), but don't you eat up mine (on me).'

Sentences such as these, which have more than one Dative of Interest on a single verb, may be considered somewhat awkward by some speakers, but they are grammatical. Their grammaticality has now been explained.

There are sentences with more than two clitic pronouns which the grammar of Spanish would generate if (86) did not filter them out, but which turn out to be ungrammatical. These cases are interesting because the *form* of the constraint (86), dictated by the proposed universal (89), *explains* why these sentences are not grammatical in Spanish.

The sentence (96) is fully grammatical, but if *Miguel* and *mí* are interchanged in the deep structure of (96), an ungrammatical sentence results.

(97)   a. *Te me comiste el pan a mí, pero a Miguel no te le lo comas.

  b. *Te me comiste el pan a mí, pero a Miguel no te se lo comas.
'You ate up my bread (on me), but don't you eat up Miguel's (on him).'

*(97a) is ungrammatical because of the pronoun sequence *le lo*; the spurious *se* rule should apply to such sequences. But application of the spurious *se* rule produces the sequence *te se lo*. Now, on the basis of the grammaticality of sentences like

(98)   Se te perdió la llave.
'The key got lost on you.'

se and *te* have been assigned to two different columns of (86), with *se* preceding *te*. The universal notation used in (86) entails that any sentence with the clitic sequence *te se lo* will be ungrammatical. (89), which requires

---

extremely strong evidence for a surface structure constraint on the clitic pronouns, since it would be unnatural, if not impossible, to constrain the transformations in such a way that a sequence of more than two clitic pronouns would never be produced. It is interesting that even though no sentences with sequences of more than two clitics are considered fully grammatical in this dialect, those which (86) predicts to be grammatical are much more acceptable than those which (86) rejects as ungrammatical. Even this dialect can therefore be said to add some confirmatory evidence to the notation of (86), although in this dialect some additional constraints appear to be operative.

29 I am indebted to Carlos Otero for this example.

the use of this notation, therefore *explains* why *(97b) is ungrammatical—why (96) is no longer grammatical if *Miguel* and *mí* are interchanged in its deep structure.

The proposed universal (89) receives further empirical support in Spanish from sentences like

> **(99)** Ramón le complicó la vida a mi hija, pero a mi hijo no se la complicó.
> 'Ramón complicated my daughter's life, but he didn't complicate my son's.'

Se la in the second half of (99) is derived from *le la* by the spurious *se* rule. This sentence can also occur with a first person singular Dative of Interest:

> **(100)** Ramón me le complicó la vida a mi hija.
> 'Ramón complicated my daughter's life on me.'

But if this Dative of Interest is added to both halves of (99), an ungrammatical sentence results.

> **(101)** a. *Ramón me le complicó la vida a mi hija, pero a mi hijo no me le la complicó.
> b. *Ramón me le complicó la vida a mi hija, pero a mi hijo no me se la complicó.
> 'Ramón complicated my daughter's life on me, but he didn't complicate my son's (on me).'

In *(101a) the spurious *se* rule has failed to apply, resulting in an ungrammatical sentence. *(101b) has the pronoun sequence *me se la,* which *a priori* there is no reason to consider ungrammatical. But the notation supplied by universal grammar, together with the actual contents of (86) in Spanish, which were motivated by entirely independent considerations, predicts that any surface structure with *me se la* will be ungrammatical. The proposed universal (89), which requires the use of this notation, thus explains why it is that adding a first person singular Dative of Interest to (99) results in an ungrammatical sentence.[30] The correctness of this prediction lends further empirical support to the proposed universal.

Recall the restrictions on the use of the clitic forms of Spanish pronouns discussed in section 2.1. For example, certain sentences with a second person Dative of Interest and a first person reflexive Dative of Interest are ungrammatical, and there are sentences in which the weak form of the indirect object pronoun can not be used if the indirect object is second person singular and the direct object is first person. In the absence of any kind of universal linguistic theory that would lead us to expect such restrictions, these constraints could only be described as bizarre. An adequate theory of language must explain why we find restrictions of precisely this

---

30 The sentence *Ramón me le complicó la vida a mi hija, pero a mi hijo no se la complicó* is of course grammatical, because it does not run afoul of (86). But this sentence does not contain a first person singular Dative of Interest in the second half, and is therefore not the sentence under discussion.

kind. A theory that includes (89) does just this. The restrictions mentioned above are co-occurrence restrictions on clitic pronouns of the type that can be expressed in the notation of (86). Since (89) states that surface structure constraints on clitics must be stated in the notation of (86), it predicts that restrictions on clitics like those mentioned above will be found in human languages.

3.5.2. The Surface Structure Constraint on Clitics in French. With (89) and (90) in universal grammar, we approach the study of other languages with an explanatory hypothesis to be tested. We expect there to be surface structure constraints on the relative order of clitics, and we expect these constraints to be statable in the notation of (86). More important, (89) and (90) predict that stating constraints on the relative order of clitics in this way will explain facts in particular languages that would otherwise be anomalous. In the study of other languages, we will find restrictions on the grammaticality of sentences with clitics which, in the absence of any kind of universal linguistic theory, would be completely mysterious. Our universals predict, however, that certain generalizations will emerge from these restrictions on the use of clitics, and that these generalizations will be of a particular type; if (89) and (90) are the only principles of universal grammar that govern the syntactic behavior of clitics,[31] universal grammar predicts that the only generalizations that will be found to underlie restrictions on the grammatical use of clitics in language after language will be the kinds of generalizations that can be captured by surface structure constraints expressed in the proposed universal notation.

In order to understand the explanatory power of universals like (89) and (90), it is necessary to put some distance between oneself and the data in a particular language. In the absence of any kind of universal linguistic theory, the data is bizarre. Consider French as an example. A pronominal indirect object of verbs like *recommander* 'recommend' may in general appear in the strong form only under contrast.

(102)   Roger l'avait recommandé à toi, pas à Jean.
        'Roger had recommended it to you, not to Jean.'

In (102) the indirect object *à toi* is being contrasted with another noun phrase. If it is not being contrasted, the weak or clitic form of the indirect object must be used.

(103)   Roger te l'avait recommandé.
        'Roger had recommended it to you.'

But if we take a sentence like

(104)   Roger nous avait recommandés à toi.
        'Roger had recommended us to you.'

---

31 It is of course not known at present whether or not there are any other such universal principles.

the strong form indirect object is not necessarily contrastive. In this example, it is impossible to use the weak or clitic form of the indirect object.

(105)   a. *Roger nous t'avait recommandés.
        b. *Roger te nous avait recommandés.

Continuing along these lines, we observe that in a sentence with a third person direct object, the indirect object *vous* can appear in the strong form only under contrast.

(106)   Roger les avait recommandés à vous, pas à Jean.
        'Roger had recommended them to you, not to Jean.'

Otherwise the clitic form is used.

(107)   Roger vous les avait recommandés.
        'Roger had recommended them to you.'

If the direct object is first person, however, only the strong form of the indirect object is possible.

(108)   Roger m'avait recommandé à vous.
        'Roger had recommended me to you.'

(109)   a. *Roger vous m'avait recommandé.
        b. *Roger me vous avait recommandé.

Similarly, a first person indirect object can appear in the weak or clitic form if there is no direct object at all, or if the direct object is third person. But if the direct object is second person, using the clitic form of a first person indirect object results in an ungrammatical sentence.

    Aren't these facts bizarre? Why, for example, should there be any restrictions at all on the regular alternation between the strong and weak forms of pronouns? (90) answers this question. It states that the clitic pronouns will be subject to a surface structure constraint, thereby predicting first, the possibility of restrictions on the otherwise regular alternation of strong and weak forms, and second, that if there are such restrictions, it will be the weak or clitic forms that are subject to them. (89), on the other hand, predicts that certain generalizations will emerge from otherwise bizarre restrictions on the use of clitic forms and that the generalizations that will emerge are the kinds that are expressable in the notation of (86).

    The generalization that underlies the observed irregularities in the alternation between the strong and weak forms of indirect objects of *recommander* can be stated as follows:

(110)   The object pronouns *me, te, nous,* and *vous* can not co-occur in the same clitic group.

Recall the discussion in section 3.4.1 of the predictions made by (89). It was pointed out there that one way to test this proposed universal would be to determine whether generalizations of the form "*the clitics A, B, and C are mutually exclusive*" would emerge from data on clitics in other languages. (110) is an example of just such a generalization. The notation of (86) provides the means of capturing this generalization in the grammar of French: these four pronouns occupy the same column in the surface structure constraint on clitics. The constraint will therefore reject as ungrammatical any sentence with more than one clitic from this set in the same clitic group. I have no explanation for the fact that in (104) and (108) the use of the strong form of the pronoun does not necessarily make the sentence contrastive. In a proper theory of language, this would presumably follow from the ungrammaticality of *(105) and *(109). However, it is not clear how this result is to be achieved. What is relevant for the present discussion is simply the fact that the ungrammaticality of *(105) and *(109) is an instance of the generalization (110), which is the type of generalization (89) predicts will be found in natural language.

With these four clitics in the same column of the French surface structure constraint, we now expect to find equally "bizarre" data elsewhere in French. That is, there should be gaps in otherwise regular paradigms from which there again will emerge the generalization that the clitics *me*, *te*, *nous*, and *vous* cannot co-occur.

There is another grammatical alternation which involves the clitic pronouns in sentences with *laisser* and a few other verbs which take infinitival complements. The sentence

(111) Je t'ai laissé les voir.
'I let you see them.'

has an alternate form in which the clitic pronoun from the embedded sentence moves up to the verb in the matrix sentence to produce the sentence [32]

(112) Je te les ai laissé voir.
'I let you see them.'

But if the matrix-sentence clitic and the clitic in the embedded sentence are both drawn from the set consisting of *me*, *te*, *nous*, and *vous*, as in

(113) Je t'ai laissé nous voir.
'I let you see us.'

then, if the embedded clitic moves up to the matrix verb, an ungrammatical sentence is produced.

(114) a. *Je te nous ai laissé voir.
b. *Je nous t'ai laissé voir.

This fact, which would otherwise be bizarre, is exactly what we expect to find if *me*, *te*, *nous*, and *vous* occupy the same column in the surface structure constraint on clitics in French.

---

[32] Within a transformational framework, these constructions are discussed by Langacker (1966) and Kayne (1969). The latter work became available to me only after this chapter had been written.

The same generalization emerges from consideration of sentences with verbs such as *se rappeler* 'remember' which are accompanied by an obligatory reflexive pronoun. In sentences like

(115)   Je me rappelle Jean-Pierre.
'I remember Jean-Pierre.'

the reflexive pronoun *me* is obligatory. If, instead of *Jean-Pierre,* the object is a third person singular masculine pronoun, we do not get

(116)   *Je me rappelle lui.

because a pronominal direct object must move to preverbal position. This produces the grammatical sentence

(117)   Je me le rappelle.
'I remember him.'

Now, if the direct object is *vous* instead of *le,* no grammatical sentence is possible.

(118)   *Je me rappelle vous.
'I remember you.'

*(118) is ungrammatical for the same reason that *(116) is; a pronominal object must move to preverbal position.[33] In this case, however, movement to preverbal position produces another ungrammatical sentence.

(119)   *Je me vous rappelle.

*(119) is ungrammatical because the clitic pronouns *me* and *vous* co-occur. *se rappeler* cannot have a second person object if the subject is first person, or a first person object if the subject is second person. These examples are all instances of the generalization (110).

Recall the discussion of positive versus negative notation in section 3.2. The positive notation was adopted primarily because it automatically accounted for the ungrammaticality of sentences with the clitic sequence *se se* in Spanish. With (89), the universality of this notation was posited. The generalization (110) in French now provides further support for the positive notation. If the negative notation had been adopted, this generalization would be unstatable. *me* and *nous* could be abbreviated as *I* (first person), and *te* and *vous* as *II* (second person), but it would still be necessary to list ungrammatical clitic pairs in the following way:

(120)   *I   II
            *II   I

---

[33] Some speakers find these sentences acceptable if some additional context is added, as in *Je me rappelle vous dans un beau costume de bain* or *Je me rappelle vous, quand vous aviez quinze ans.* This is only of marginal interest here, however, since our chief concern is with the ungrammaticality of certain sequences of clitic pronouns, as exemplified by *(119).

That is, it would be necessary to make two separate statements: that *II* cannot follow *I* and that it cannot precede it. In the negative notation, there is no way to capture the generalization that they cannot co-occur.[34]

We can now proceed to construct the chart that states the surface structure constraint on clitics in French. The clitics which agglutinate to the verb include not only the object pronouns, but also the negative particle *ne* and the subject pronouns. Except in nonnegative imperatives, the entire group of clitics precedes the verb.[35] Noting which *pairs* of clitics co-occur, we construct the following chart in the notation of (86):

(121)   Surface structure constraint on clitics:

		me				
Nom	*ne*	te	III	III	*y*	*en*
		nous	Acc	Dat		
		vous				
		se				

---

34 The positive notation that (89) predicts will be appropriate in all languages not only can capture this generalization, but, in so doing, it also correctly predicts that the clitic sequences *I I* and *II II* will be ungrammatical in French. However, it is not clear whether or not sentences with these clitic sequences will be ruled out by syntactic or semantic constraints that are needed independently of any surface structure considerations.

35 In nonnegative imperatives the relative order of the clitics is different as well, with the first and second person object pronouns following the third person Accusative pronouns. These facts could be handled in either of two ways. The first would be to subject nonnegative imperatives to a different surface structure constraint than applies to other sentences of French. The second would be to postulate a transformation which rearranges the clitics after the surface structure constraint has applied. This rule would presumably interchange a first or second person clitic with a third person clitic in nonnegative imperatives. (Another possibility would be to consider the order found in nonnegative imperatives as the basic order specified by the surface structure constraint, and postulate a rule that interchanges a first or second person clitic with a third person clitic in all other sentences. This variant of the second possibility mentioned above does not affect the point being made here.) In choosing between these two possibilities, we should note that the first one, which posits two separate surface structure constraints on clitics in French, fails to capture the fact that the two constraints are essentially the same. For example, the generalizaion (110) holds in nonnegative imperatives as well as in other sentences, since the assignment of individual clitics to columns of the surface constraint chart would be the same for both constraints. The only difference is the position of *me*/*te*/*nous*/*vous* relative to third person clitics. The relevant generalizations can be captured by means of the second possibility mentioned above, which posits a clitic flip rule following the application of the surface structure constraint, but they would be missed by the first alternative. Since the evidence in French is somewhat inconclusive, we will not pursue this question further here. If the second possibility mentioned above is indeed correct, however, it shows that surface structure constraints on clitics do not necessarily apply to the final output generated by the grammar, since there can be rules which apply after them. This would make it necessary to discover just what types of rules can apply after the application of surface structure constraints, constraining this class of rules as much as possible. It would also mean that, if the term "surface structure" denotes the output of the last transformation, surface structure constraints will have to seek a new name.

Here the symbol "Nom" abbreviates the set of subject pronouns *je, tu, il, elle, nous, vous, ils, elles, on*; "III Acc" abbreviates the set *le, la, les*; and "III Dat" abbreviates the set *lui, leur*.

The third person reflexive pronoun *se* has been included in the same column of (121) as *me, te, nous,* and *vous* because it cannot co-occur with any of these clitic pronouns. This can be illustrated by sentences with *se rappeler* 'remember'.

(122) Il se le rappelle.
'He remembers him.'

is grammatical, but if *se rappeler* has a third person subject, the object cannot be first or second person.

(123) a. *Il se me rappelle.
'He remembers me.'
b. *Il se te rappelle.
'He remembers you.'
c. *Il se nous rappelle.
'He remembers us.'
d. *Il se vous rappelle.
'He remembers you.'

The chart (121) is, of course, well known, and has been included in many grammars of French. However, to my knowledge, no theory has been advanced to explain why the constraints on the relative order of clitics in French should be stated in a chart of this form rather than in some other way. If (89) and (90) are included in linguistic theory, then linguistic theory will have provided such an explanation. The correct predictions that (121) makes about grammaticality in French constitute empirical evidence in support of the proposed universals, while at the same time these proposed universals constitute an explanatory theory that explains why we find the kind of facts that we do in French.

A second way this proposal differs from traditional treatments of clitics in French is that it is made explicit that the chart (121) performs a filtering function, rejecting as ungrammatical any sentence generated by the transformational component in which the clitic group does not conform to it. It is necessary to regard (121) as a filter in order to account for the ungrammaticality of sentences like *(119) and *(123). Some other treatment, such as one that proposes rules to rearrange the clitics into the correct order, would be inadequate because the sentence contains two incompatible clitics; these sentences will be ungrammatical, no matter what the relative order of the clitics. In the other examples we have considered, regarding (121) as a filter makes it unnecessary to place special ad hoc constraints on transformations to prevent the generation of ungrammatical sentences.

With (121), motivated by linguistic universals, in the grammar of French, it is now possible to *explain* certain facts noted by Gross (1968). Gross points out that in a sentence like

(124) Il remplit un verre de ce vin.
'He fills a glass with this wine.'

both complements of the verb can be sources of the pro-form *en*. That is, we get both

(125) Il en remplit un verre.
'He fills a glass with it.'

and

(126) Il en remplit un de ce vin.
'He fills one with this wine.'

But both complements can not be replaced by *en* in the same sentence.

(127) *Il en en remplit un.

This fact follows automatically from the proposed universals (89) and (90) and the inclusion of *en* in only one column of (121).

Similarly, Gross points out that while *dans cette chambre* can be replaced by the pro-form *y*, as in

(128) a. Jean réfléchit dans cette chambre.
'Jean thinks in this room.'
b. Jean y réfléchit.
'Jean thinks there.'

and although nonhuman objects of *à* can likewise be replaced by *y*, as in

(129) a. Jean réfléchit à cet événement.
'Jean is thinking about this event.'
b. Jean y réfléchit.
'Jean is thinking about it.'

dans cette chambre and *à cet événement* cannot both be replaced by *y* in the same sentence.

(130) a. Jean réfléchit à cet événement, dans cette chambre.
'Jean is thinking about this event in this room.'
b. *Jean y y réfléchit.

This fact likewise follows automatically from the proposed universals (89) and (90) and the inclusion of *y* in only one column of (121).

It might be tempting to try to ascribe the ungrammaticality of clitic sequences like *en en* and *y y* to some kind of a theory of "euphony." Such a theory might also be invoked to explain why *se rappeler* can not have a reflexive object. It has already been seen that there is reason to abandon the attempt to account for the ungrammaticality of *se se* and *le le* in Spanish on phonological grounds. An attempt to account for the ungrammaticality of *en en* and *y y* in French on phonological grounds would likewise be misguided in two respects. First, only a fraction of the ungrammatical clitic sequences in French consist of repeated elements such as *en en* and *y y*.

The theory of surface structure constraints expressed in the notation of (121) is needed anyway to account for other examples, and since this theory automatically accounts for these cases as well, there is no need for a theory of "euphony." Second, a theory of "euphony" would require that ungrammatical sequences of pronouns be characterizable in terms of phonological shape. Such a theory might attempt to explain the fact that sequences of object pronouns like *nous nous, vous vous,* and so on are ungrammatical in terms of the repetition of the same phonological shape. Such a theory would necessarily fail, however, because these pronoun sequences are ungrammatical only if both pronouns are object pronouns. If one is a subject pronoun and the other an object pronoun, these sequences are perfectly grammatical.

> **(131)** Nous nous rappelons qu'elle avait les yeux bleus.
> 'We remember that she had blue eyes.'

> **(132)** Est-ce que vous vous rappelez son sourire à moitié caché?
> 'Do you remember her half-hidden smile?'

The grammaticality of these sentences shows that in those cases where *nous nous* and *vous vous* sequences are ungrammatical it is because they are both object pronouns, and they are allotted only one column in (121). Their phonological shape has nothing to do with the ungrammaticality. The same phonological sequence is perfectly grammatical if one pronoun is a subject pronoun and the other an object pronoun, for subject and object pronouns occupy different columns of (121).[36]

In section 3.5, it has been seen that (89) and (90) make a number of additional correct predictions. The interpretation given to the notation of (86), which (89) posits as universal, makes correct predictions about sequences of more than two clitics in Spanish. (89) and (90) together predict that in other languages there will be restrictions on the co-occurrence of clitics of a particular kind. Data of exactly the predicted kind has been found in French.

3.6. Further Problems

3.6.1. Nonglobal Constraints on Clitics.
The constraints (86) and (121) have been shown to be necessary in the grammars of Spanish and French to filter out certain ungrammatical sentences that would otherwise be generated by the transformational component. The notation in which they are stated has been justified, and it has been shown that constraints stated in this notation make a number of correct predictions that go beyond

---

36 This shows that the third column of (121) must be identified as consisting of *object* pronouns. The problem of how this is to be done, and how the constraint is actually to be applied to sentences so that (131) and (132) are not filtered out while sentences with two successive first or second person object pronouns *are* filtered out, will not be discussed further here.

the data which originally motivated them. Section 3.6.1 deals with certain ungrammatical sentences that might at first be thought to constitute counter-evidence to the notation proposed here.

Since it has been claimed that (86) and (121) act as filters of the output of the transformational component, the existence of any grammatical sentences in Spanish or French with clitic sequences which (86) or (121) would filter out would constitute counterevidence to the theory developed here. It is a very different matter, however, to ask whether *all* sentences with clitic sequences that (86) and (121) allow will be grammatical. To take an extreme example, consider a nonsentence of French like

> **(133)**   *Je ne se les leur y en pense.

(121) will not filter out *(133) as ungrammatical, but its ungrammaticality is beyond question. The ungrammaticality of *(133) not only cannot be due to (121), it has nothing whatever to do with the problem of clitics; putting as many of the clitics in *(133) as possible in the corresponding strong forms would not make the sentence grammatical. Quite simply, there is no underlying structure which the transformational component would convert into *(133). This example should make it clear that the existence of an ungrammatical sentence with a clitic sequence that (86) or (121) would not filter out would not necessarily constitute counterevidence to the theory developed here.

It is a more interesting question to ask whether, in the absence of any constraints on clitics other than (86) and (121), the grammars of Spanish and French will generate any ungrammatical sentences with clitic sequences that (86) and (121) do not filter out. If there is evidence that the ungrammaticality of these sentences is due to the clitic sequences they contain, and if the same clitic sequences are grammatical in other constructions, one can tentatively conclude that their ungrammaticality is due to construction-particular or *nonglobal constraints* on clitics. Such nonglobal constraints would be additional constraints, superimposed on the *global constraints* (86) and (121), which set an upper limit on grammatical sequences of clitics in Spanish and French.

Spanish provides some evidence for the existence of such nonglobal constraints on clitics. Consider, first, clitic sequences in sentences with *recomendar*. If the direct object is third person, the clitic form of the indirect object may be used freely.

> **(134)**   a.   Me lo recomendaron.
>   'They recommended him to me.'
>   b.   Te lo recomendaron.
>   'They recommended him to you.'
>   c.   Se lo recomendaron.
>   'They recommended him to him/her/them.'

But if the direct object is first or second person and the indirect object is third person, the clitic form of the indirect object can not be used.

(135) a. *Me le recomendaron.
'They recommended me to him.'
b. *Te le recomendaron.
'They recommended you to him.'

To express *(135) in Spanish, it is necessary to use the strong form of the indirect object.

(136) a. Me recomendaron a él.
'They recommended me to him.'
b. Te recomendaron a él.
'They recommended you to him.'

The *me le* and *te le* sequences of *(135) result in ungrammatical sentences. Yet, the clitic sequences *me le* and *te le* are perfectly grammatical in

(137) a. Me le escapé.
'I escaped from him.'
b. Te le escapaste.
'You escaped from him.'

and

(138) a. Me le acerqué.
'I approached (to) him.'
b. Te le acercaste.
'You approached (to) him.'

as well as in sentences with two Datives of Interest.

(139) Ramón me le complicó la vida a mi hija.
'Ramón complicated my daughter's life on me.'

The ungrammaticality of *(135) must be due to the use of the clitic form of the indirect object, since use of the corresponding strong form in (136) results in a grammatical sentence. It is necessary to conclude that some nonglobal constraint involving clitics is responsible for the ungrammaticality of *(135).

For some speakers, the constraint responsible for the ungrammaticality of *(135) is more general, and can be stated approximately as follows:

(140) If the direct object of *recomendar* is first or second person, use of the clitic form of the indirect object results in an ungrammatical sentence.[37]

These speakers do not accept sentences like

(141) Te me recomendaron.
'They recommended me to you; they recommended you to me.'

---

[37] (140) certainly applies to a wider class of cases than just objects of *recomendar*, but the problem of determining the range of cases to which it applies does not concern us here.

which other speakers find grammatical. This situation is rather typical of nonglobal constraints on clitics, which are subject to a great deal of dialectal variation.

The *reflexivum tantum* construction of (137) provides another example of a nonglobal constraint on clitics in Spanish. For all speakers I have asked, the clitics in this construction must come in the order specified by (86). Some speakers have the additional constraint that the obligatory reflexive pronoun must precede the nonreflexive Dative of Interest. They accept

(142) Te me escapaste.
'You escaped from me.'

in which the reflexive *te* precedes the nonreflexive *me,* but not

(143) *Te me escapé.
'I escaped from you.'

because in *(143) the clitic order that conforms to (86) entails that the nonreflexive *te* must precede the reflexive *me.*[38] Other speakers lack the constraint that the reflexive clitic must precede the nonreflexive one, and they consequently find both (142) and (143) grammatical.

French also provides an example of a nonglobal constraint on clitics. *me/te/nous/vous/se* and *lui/leur* were assigned to different columns of (121), because the first set can only precede *le/la/les* and the second set can only follow them.[39] However, in sentences with *recommander,* if the direct object is first or second person, the use of the strong form of a third person indirect object is grammatical and noncontrastive.

(144) Ton cousin m'a recommandé à lui.
'Your cousin recommended me to him.'

Use of the clitic form of the indirect object results in an ungrammatical sentence.[40]

(145) *Ton cousin me lui a recommandé.

Similarly, the sentence

(146) Tes cousins m'ont laissé lui parler.
'Your cousins let me speak to him.'

should have an alternate form like (112) in which the clitics from the embedded sentence have moved up into the matrix sentence. However, the result

---

38 Recall that subject pronouns in Spanish are deleted by a late rule. Since the subject of (142) is the second person singular *tú,* in (142) *te* is reflexive and *me* is nonreflexive. The subject of *(143), on the other hand, is the first person singular *yo.* As a result, *me* in *(143) is reflexive, while *te* is nonreflexive.

39 Except for nonnegative imperatives, as noted in footnote 35.

40 This fact suggests that (110) may be but a subcase of a broader generalization, which might be the same as (140) in Spanish.

(147) *Tes cousins me lui ont laissé parler.

is ungrammatical. What *(145) and *(147) have in common is the clitic sequence *me lui*. Since (121) does not filter these sentences out, their ungrammaticality is unaccounted for. It might be due to a nonglobal constraint on clitics. To show this, it is necessary to show that there are grammatical sentences of French that have the clitic sequence *me lui*. There is, in fact, such a class of sentences. While their status may be somewhat marginal for some speakers, others accept them. These are sentences like

(148) Tu vas me lui écrire cette lettre!
'You will write him that letter (for me)!'

(149) Tu vas me lui obéir!
'You will obey him (for me)!'

Again, the English translations are only approximate. (148) and (149) have imperative force, and the *me* in each sentence is an Ethical Dative. Sentences of this type are grammatical even if the subject is third person, as long as there is a certain connection between the subject of the sentence and the person at whom it is directed.

(150) Ton frère va me lui obéir!
'Your brother will obey him (for me)!'

The grammaticality of (148–150) shows that we cannot let (121) filter out sentences with *me lui*, even if this were possible by means of a different interpretation of the notation. Furthermore, even imperative-force sentences with a first person singular Ethical Dative are ungrammatical if they contain the clitic sequence *me te* or *te me*.

(151) a. *Ton frère va me t'obéir!
    b. *Ton frère va te m'obéir!
    'Your brother will obey you (for me)!'

*(151) will be filtered out by (121), as predicted. At the same time, (121) will not reject *(145), *(147), or (148–150). Since (148–150) must pass through the filter as grammatical sentences, it is necessary to conclude that the ungrammaticality of *(145) and *(147) is due to a nonglobal constraint on clitics.

It has been the purpose of section 3.6.1 to show that nonglobal constraints on clitics exist, and that their existence does not compromise the validity of (86) and (121) or of the notation used to state them. Of course, a theory that automatically predicted the nonglobal constraints on clitics to be found in each language at the same time that it accounted for the phenomena that (86) and (121) account for would be preferable to the theory developed here. The examples presented here, however, show this possibility to be rather unlikely. Adequate grammars of Spanish and French will have to include certain nonglobal constraints on clitics in addition to (86) and (121). Questions of the range of phenomena to which they apply, of whether they are transformational or surface structure constraints, and of the way they are to be stated in grammars will be left open here.

3.6.2. A Possible Explanation for (89) and (90). It has been seen that (89) and (90) explain a number of phenomena involving clitics in Spanish and French. But it is also necessary to seek an explanation for (89) and (90) themselves. Why should clitics be universally subject to surface structure constraints, rather than manner adverbials, verbs of mental activity, or mass nouns? And why should a notation like ours be the appropriate mechanism for stating these constraints? A partial answer to these questions may come from the fact that clitics form a single phonological word with the word they attach to. In French and Spanish, this is the verb. In some languages, such as Serbo-Croatian and Walbiri, clitics move to "second position" in the sentence, where they form a single word with the previous word, whatever it is. This parasitic behavior of clitics at the word level is what defines them as clitics. It should, therefore, not be surprising if an explanation for their being subject to surface structure constraints were to follow from their basic, defining property. And there seems not to be any serious counterevidence to the generalization, pointed out to me by Paul Postal, that within the word the order of morphemes is fixed in all languages. That is, if there are two words which contain the same morphemes but in a different order, then the underlying representations of the two are distinct.[41] This entails that whereas many languages have phenomena like "free word order," there are no languages in which the order of morphemes within the word is free.[42] Since clitics form a single word with the word on which they lean, the fact that their relative order is fixed may be but a special case of the fixed order of morphemes within the word. This suggests that the word may universally be subject to surface structure constraints on the relative order of its component morphemes, and that the notation developed here may be appropriate for stating those constraints. If this is so, (89) and (90) would follow from a principle something like

(152)   The word is universally subject to surface structure constraints on morpheme order, and these constraints are expressed in the notation of (86) and (121).

---

41 French imperatives, discussed briefly in footnote 35, show that this formulation is only approximate. While the underlying structures of imperative and nonimperative sentences are certainly distinct, it is likely that in underlying representations the distinction is not marked *on those morphemes that end up as the imperative-form verb and the clitics attached to it.*

42 The possibility of clitic flip rules following the application of a surface structure constraint has been noted in footnote 35. If there are examples of this, and if other constraints on clitics are a consequence of order constraints within the word, then we would expect to find cases of similar morpheme flip rules within the word. I do not know whether or not such rules exist.

It remains to be seen whether a principle as strong as (152) survives empirical test.

If constraints on clitic order follow from the fact that clitics form a single word with the constituent they attach to, this may also explain certain other facts about the verb-plus-clitics group. One cannot put a major pause between clitics, or between the clitics and the verb. This should follow automatically from the fact that one cannot put a major pause in the middle of a word. Similarly, adverbs and parenthetical expressions can not be inserted between clitics.

> (153)   a.   Je lui en ai parlé.
>   'I spoke to him about it.'
>   b.   *Je lui souvent en ai parlé.
>   'I often spoke to him about it.'

or beween clitics and the verb [43]

> (154)   a.   Jean-Pierre, si je me souviens bien, boit de la bière.
>   'Jean-Pierre, if I remember correctly, drinks beer.'
>   b.   *Il, si je me souviens bien, boit de la bière.
>   'He, if I remember correctly, drinks beer.'

The latter fact can be made to follow from our notation, which would discard any sentence with something intervening among the allowed elements in a chart like (86) or (121). To do this, it would only be necessary to add the element "Verb" to the right-hand end of (86) and (121). However, it is not clear whether this fact *should* be accounted for by means of this notation. Perhaps it should be accounted for in the same way that we account for the impossibility of pauses within the verb-plus-clitics group. This suggests again that the notation we have proposed may be but a special case of a greater generalization concerning syntactic properties of the word.

3.6.3. Other Constraints Statable in the Proposed Notation. If the use of our notation to state surface structure constraints on clitic order is a special case of its being used to state morpheme order constraints within the word, the question naturally arises of whether grammars use this notation only for phenomena within the word. There are some indications that this is not the case. Consider, for example, the constituents of the English noun phrase, as in

> (155)   all the lovely narrow red brick houses

If (155) is taken to be a chart in the notation of (86) and (121), and if the noun *houses* is made obligatory, all the combinations of elements

---

[43] The fact that adverbs and parenthetical expressions cannot be inserted after pronominal subjects and after the negative particle *ne*, just as they can not be inserted among the other clitics or between the clitics and the verb, is evidence that subject pronouns and *ne*, in fact, *are* clitics in French. Additional evidence for this is given in Kayne (1969).

predicted by our notation are grammatical and all others are ungrammatical. Thus there are grammatical noun phrases like

(156)   a. all the red brick houses
        b. the lovely narrow houses
        c. all narrow brick houses
        d. all the red houses

and many others. But if any of the elements of (155) are put in a different order, the result is ungrammatical.

(157)   a. *red the houses
        b. *red lovely houses
        c. *narrow all houses
        d. *all the lovely red narrow brick houses

If the notation of (86) and (121) is indeed necessary to state the constraints on the order of constituents in the English noun phrase, then this would constitute evidence that this phenomenon is also a surface structure constraint. It would then be necessary to replace (155) by a chart in which each column indicates the full range of constituents which occupy that position in the noun phrase.[44]

It should be clear that while it is claimed that the notation of (86) and (121) is universal for the statement of surface structure constraints on clitics, and while this notation may have other uses as well, it is not claimed that all surface structure constraints are to be stated in this notation. There may well be other types of surface structure constraints which are to be stated differently.

3.7. Summary

It has been my purpose in this section to propose a universal notation for the statement of surface structure constraints on the relative order of clitics. On the basis of certain facts of Spanish, I have proposed that a

---

44 Vendler (1968) does essentially this. His proposed constraint on the order of adjectives in English can be expressed in the chart notation of (86) and (121), with each column of the chart occupied by a class of adjectives. These classes of adjectives are defined by Vendler on the basis of a number of interesting syntactic and semantic properties. See also Hill (1958, 175–190), where similar examples are given and discussed in some detail.

Actually, the facts are somewhat more complicated if we consider the problem of adverb occurrence within the noun phrase. Adverbs can occur inside (155) in phrases like *the lovely bright red incredibly narrow brick houses*. The crucial point here is that *bright red* forms a single constituent, as does *incredibly narrow*. The only adverbs that can precede an adjective here are its modifiers. This suggests that the columns of an adequate statement of the relative order constraint on constituents of the English noun phrase must represent not just classes of adjectives, but rather adjectives with their modifiers, with the further constraint that the modifiers must precede the adjectives. External elements, such as sentence adverbs, cannot occur inside the noun phrase and would be excluded by our notation.

proper theory of language will have to include (89) and (90). That is, linguistic theory will have to posit the existence of surface structure constraints on clitics and the notation proposed here to state them as universals of human language. I then went on to show that a linguistic theory which does this will automatically account for a number of additional facts of Spanish, as well as explain certain phenomena in French which would otherwise be quite bizarre. By showing the explanatory power of a linguistic theory·which incorporates (89) and (90) in some way, I have attempted to illustrate the subtle interplay between language-particular facts and linguistic universals of which the grammars of natural languages are constructed. At first glance, one might suppose that nothing could be more language-particular than the constraints on the relative order of clitic pronouns in Spanish, all the more so because the constraint must refer to such language-particular entities as the morpheme *se*. Yet the universals that the Spanish data lead one to propose succeed in explaining a number of additional facts in both Spanish and French, while these facts lend further empirical support to the proposed universals. Most important, I have tried to show that in the absence of any universal linguistic theory, one is confronted with data in natural languages that can only be described as bizarre. Once linguistic universals capable of explaining the facts have been formulated, facts which were at first bizarre are seen to be completely regular.

4. EVIDENCE THAT THE CONSTRAINT IN SPANISH IS STATABLE ONLY AS A SURFACE STRUCTURE CONSTRAINT

In section 2, empirical motivation was given for a constraint to filter out sentences with certain sequences of object pronouns in surface structure. In section 3, the form that the statement of this constraint should take was discussed. However, it has not yet been shown that the constraints on the relative order of clitic pronouns in Spanish can not be stated in some other way. In section 4, it will be shown, first, that these constraints can not be stated transformationally, and second, that they can not be stated by means of the phrase structure rules of the base component.

4.1. Evidence that the Constraint Cannot Be Stated Transformationally

There are two conceivable ways of stating the constraint on the order of clitic pronouns in Spanish transformationally. The first would be to regard the chart (86) as the structural change of a clitic-reordering transformation. Under this proposal, there would be a rule which takes all the clitic pronouns in the sentence and rearranges them into the order dictated by (86). Another possibility would be to postulate a series of transformations whose effect would be to arrange the clitics in the order specified by (86). We will deal with the former alternative first.

If (86) is not a surface structure constraint, but rather the structural change of a clitic-reordering transformation, then clitic-reordering, being a rule in the grammar of Spanish, would have to be ordered with respect to other rules. In particular, it would have to be ordered with respect to the spurious *se* rule. But ordering clitic-reordering either before or after the spurious *se* rule results in an inadequate grammar.

If (86) is to be the structural change of a clitic-reordering transformation which precedes the spurious *se* rule, it must be changed slightly and restated as:

(158)   S.C. of clitic-reordering transformation:

se	II	I	III	III
			Dat	Acc

This change is necessary because *le* and *les* must be allowed to precede the third person Accusative pronouns in order to derive sentences like

(159)   Se lo di a Miguel.
'I gave it to Miguel.'

where the *se* comes from *le* by means of the spurious *se* rule. Following the application of the clitic-reordering transformation (158), the spurious *se* rule will apply and yield sentences like (159). However, there is now no way to discard sentences like

(39b)   *A mí se me permitió dormir toda la mañana, pero a Sarita no se se lo ha permitido.
'I was allowed to sleep all morning, but Sarita was not allowed to.'

and

(46b)   *A los generales se les da los honores, pero a los conscriptos no se se los da.
'To the generals the honors are given, but to the draftees they are not.'

which must be ruled out because they contain *se se* sequences that came into being as a result of the application of the spurious *se* rule. We must conclude that if (86) is the structural change of a clitic-reordering transformation (restated as (158)), it cannot precede the spurious *se* rule.

If (86) is the structural change of a clitic-reordering rule that *follows* the spurious *se* rule, we fare no better. Such a clitic-reordering rule would take an ungrammatical sentence like

(97b)   *Te me comiste el pan a mí, pero a Miguel no te se lo comas.
'You ate up my bread (on me), but don't you eat up Miguel's (on him).'

and put the clitics in the "correct" order embodied in (86). A grammatical sentence should result, but the resulting sentence is ungrammatical:

(160)   *Te me comiste el pan a mí, pero a Miguel no se te lo comas.

By the same token, if (86) is the structural change of a clitic-reordering transformation, it should operate on

(101b) *Ramón me le complicó la vida a mi hija, pero a mi hijo no me se la complicó.
'Ramón complicated my daughter's life on me, but he didn't complicate my son's (on me).'

to produce a grammatical sentence. But the result

(161b) *Ramón me le complicó la vida a mi hija, pero a mi hijo no se me la complicó.

is ungrammatical. It is necessary to conclude that if (86) is the structural change of a clitic-reordering transformation, it can not follow the spurious *se* rule.

For exactly the same reasons, (86) can not be the structural change of a clitic-reordering transformation of the type that Lakoff and Ross have called "anywhere rules," which can apply at any point in derivations at which their structural description is met. For if this were the case, *(160) and *(161) would be grammatical, and they are not.

If (86) is the structural change of a clitic-reordering transformation, the transformation in question can neither precede nor follow the spurious *se* rule, nor can it be an "anywhere rule." It follows that it is not a transformation at all.

Any attempt to state the constraint on the order of clitic pronouns by means of a series of transformations of some kind whose effect would be to rearrange the clitics into the order specified by (86) would encounter exactly the same difficulties. If these transformations precede the spurious *se* rule, it is impossible to rule out the *se se* sequences produced by the spurious *se* rule, as well as to characterize as ungrammatical such sentences as *(97b) and *(101b), which have the pronoun sequences *te se lo* and *me se la* produced by the spurious *se* rule. If, on the other hand, the reordering transformations one attempts to formulate follow the spurious *se* rule, it is impossible to account for the ungrammaticality of sentences like *(160) and *(161). Any attempt to order some clitic-reordering transformations before the spurious *se* rule and others after it would still encounter the same difficulties. Sentences like *(97b) and *(101b) will be ungrammatical no matter what the order of the clitic pronouns, as the rearrangement to *(160) and *(161) shows. Similarly, sentences with the clitic sequence *se se* have to be characterized as ungrammatical, and no amount of rearrangement of the clitics can make them into grammatical sentences.

That no transformation or series of transformations can account for the data in Spanish can be seen quite strikingly in the case of those constructions that, for many speakers, have their own clitic order constraints that are independent of those embodied in the global output constraint (86). In order for a grammatical sentence to result, both constraints must be satisfied. For example, in the construction (162) the reflexive pronoun must precede the nonreflexive. When the reflexive pronoun precedes the other pronoun in the chart (86) as well, we get a grammatical sentence.

(162) a. Se nos escapó.
'He escaped from us.'
b. Te me escapaste.
'You escaped from me.'
c. Me les escapé.
'I escaped from them.'

When (86) is violated, an ungrammatical sentence results.[45]

(163) a. *Me te escapé.
'I escaped from you.'
b. *Nos te escapamos.
'We escaped from you.'

Now, if (86) were the structural change of a clitic-reordering transformation, or if there were a series of transformations that had this effect, such transformational devices would reverse the order of the pronouns in *(163) and thereby yield grammatical sentences. But the resulting sentences are ungrammatical.[46]

(164) a. *Te me escapé.
b. *Te nos escapamos.

It follows that (86) is not the structural change of a transformation or series of transformations, but rather a surface constraint which rejects sentences with certain sequences of pronouns as ungrammatical.

The attempt to state the constraint on the order of clitic pronouns in Spanish transformationally is based on the assumption that all that needs to be done to get a grammatical sentence is to arrange the clitics into the correct order. But this assumption is false. *(97b) and *(101b) show this, since their arrangement into the correct order produces the ungrammatical sentences *(160) and *(161). Sentences with the *se se* sequence —whether it arises through the application of the spurious *se* rule, as in *(39b) and *(46b), or by other means, as in *(51b) and *(62b)—also show this, since these sentences are ungrammatical and there is simply no way to make them grammatical. Finally, the sentences in *(163) and *(164) also illustrate the point that rearrangement of the clitic-pronouns by some transformational device or other is simply unable to account for all of the data. The data can be accounted for by a surface structure constraint, however, since the function of such a constraint is to filter out ungrammatical sentences. If the surface structure constraint is applied *after* the appli-

---

45 * *Me escapé a ti* and * *Nos escapamos a ti* are ungrammatical as well, because of the requirement that the Dative noun phrase be duplicated as a clitic pronoun.

46 As was pointed out in section 3.6.1, for speakers who do not require the reflexive pronoun to come first in this construction, (164) is grammatical. This argument therefore is not valid for that variety of Spanish.

cation of the spurious *se* rule, all of the ill-formed sentences discussed here will correctly be filtered out as ungrammatical.

This discussion has led to the discovery that there are well-formed deep structures to which there correspond no grammatical surface structures. This is illustrated by

(51b)   *Cuando se roba, se se arrepiente muy pronto.
'When *Pro* steals, *Pro* repents very quickly.'

and

(62b)   *Cuando se come, se se lava las manos antes.
'When *Pro* eats, *Pro* washes *Pro*'s hands beforehand.'

This is also the case with the sentences in *(163), since there are no grounds whatever for ruling out their deep structures as ill formed, and yet there is no way to actualize these deep structures as grammatical sentences. In the case of the sentences in *(163), this can be shown in a particularly striking way. Deep structures like "I escaped from you" and "We escaped from you" must be well formed in Spanish, for they underlie certain grammatical sentences. Spanish has grammatical sentences like

(165)   Te le escapaste a Jorge, pero a mí no te me escapaste.
'You escaped from Jorge, but you didn't escape from me.'

from which most of the second half of the sentence can be deleted, producing sentences like

(166)   Te le escapaste a Jorge, pero a mí no.
'You escaped from Jorge, but not from me.'

Corresponding to (166), the sentence

(167)   Me le escapé a Jorge, pero a ti no.
'I escaped from Jorge, but not from you.'

is fully grammatical. The deep structure underlying (167) must be "I escaped from Jorge, but I didn't escape from you" appropriately expressed in Spanish. In other words, the deep structure "I escaped from you" in Spanish must be well formed, for it underlies part of the grammatical sentence (167). But this deep structure by itself can never be actualized as a grammatical sentence of Spanish, because the output runs afoul of the surface structure constraint (86). Only if the part of the sentence containing the clitic pronouns has been deleted does this deep structure emerge as a grammatical sentence. This is the case in (167). This shows that the deep structure of *(163a) is well formed, and it is only the order of the clitic pronouns in surface structure that causes it to be ungrammatical. The same is true of *(163b), since the sentence

(168)   Nos le escapamos a Jorge, pero a ti no.
'We escaped from Jorge, but not from you.'

is fully grammatical. Like (167), (168) cannot be continued, for if the clitics have not been deleted there is no way to say "We escaped from you" grammatically.[47] But the deep structure of this sentence underlies the second half of (168), and therefore must be well formed. The existence of sentences like "I escaped from you," which have well-formed deep structures but cannot be actualized as grammatical sentences, is therefore the strongest kind of evidence for a surface structure constraint on the order of clitic pronouns in Spanish.

An analogous argument can be given to show that the constraint (121) in French cannot be stated transformationally. As was noted in section 3.5.2, *se rappeler* 'remember' can not have a first or second person object. Sentences like

(169) *Je me vous rappelle.
'I remember you.'

are ungrammatical. Rearranging the clitics does not help, because

(170) *Je vous me rappelle.

---

[47] There is no way to say "I escaped from you" and "We escaped from you" with the Dative of Interest, that is, using the same construction that we find in

(i) Te me escapaste.
'You escaped from me.'

There is another sentence of Spanish that would also be translated into English as "You escaped from me," but which uses a directional *de*-phrase instead of the Dative of Interest. With this construction we get

(ii) Te escapaste de mí.
'You escaped from me.'

And, alongside (ii), we can say

(iii) Me escapé de ti.
'I escaped from you.'
(iv) Nos escapamos de ti.
'We escaped from you.'

These sentences are possible because they do not violate the output constraint (86). But they are very different in meaning from the construction with the Dative of Interest, just as (ii) differs markedly in meaning from (i). This difference in meaning can perhaps be brought out by contrasting

(v) El ex-presidente le había sacado mucho dinero a la República.
'The ex-president had taken a lot of money from the Republic.'
(vi) El ex-presidente había sacado mucho dinero de la República.
'The ex-president had taken a lot of money out of the Republic.'

(v) indicates that the former president had stolen money from the Republic, although he had not necessarily taken it outside its borders. (vi), on the other hand, conveys the idea of his having taken money outside the country, but there is no intimation of his having gotten it at the expense of the Republic. (ii), like (vi), indicates a physical action. (i), on the other hand, like (v), indicates an action with respect to, or, in this case, at the expense of, the other party, although not necessarily a physical action.

is ungrammatical as well. There is simply no way to say this sentence grammatically in French, using the verb *se rappeler*.[48] Yet, we can show that the deep structure underlying *(169) is well formed, for it can emerge from the syntactic component as grammatical just in case there are other circumstances that prevent the ungrammatical clitic sequence *me vous* from arising. For example, the sentence

(171)   Je ne me rappelle ni vous ni votre frère.
'I remember neither you nor your brother.'

is perfectly grammatical, since we must use the strong form of the pronoun in a *ni . . . ni . . .* construction and the ungrammatical sequence *me vous* is not produced. Similarly, although *(169) is ungrammatical, sentences like

(172)   Je me rappelle Mireille, mais pas vous.
'I remember Mireille, but not you.'

are perfectly grammatical. The deep structure underlying (172) contains two sentences conjoined with *mais* 'but'. The structure underlying the second of these two conjoined sentences is identical to the deep structure underlying *(169), except that here negation is added. In the derivation of (172), the part of the second conjoined sentence that is identical to the first conjoined sentence is deleted in the course of the derivation. As a result, the ungrammatical pronoun sequence *me vous* does not arise. The grammaticality of (172), like that of (171), shows that the deep structure underlying *(169) is well formed; it is only the pronoun sequence *me vous* in surface structure that causes *(169) to be ungrammatical.

In section 4.1, it has been shown that in adequate grammars of Spanish and French the constraints on the order of clitic pronouns cannot be stated by means of a clitic-reordering transformation or a series of such transformations. There are sentences with well-formed deep structures that have no corresponding well-formed surface structures. The surface structure constraints (86) and (121) are needed to filter these sentences out.

This is a rather surprising result. An adequate linguistic theory must predict the possibility of finding examples of blocking of exactly this kind. A linguistic theory that did not include (89) and (90) in some form would fail to do this. Even if it is assumed that clitic order is fixed in all languages, it does not follow that there will be examples of sentences with well-formed deep structures and no well-formed surface structures. That is, *a priori*

---

[48] This statement is correct as it stands for those speakers for whom *se rappeler* cannot take an object with *de*. For these speakers, *Je me rappelle Jean-Pierre* is grammatical, but *Je me rappelle de Jean-Pierre* is not. There are other speakers of French who find both of these sentences grammatical. For this variety of French, it is not quite correct to say that *se rappeler* cannot take a first or second person object, since for these speakers sentences like *Je me rappelle de vous* and *Il se rappelle de moi* are grammatical. But even in this variety of French, it is necessary to explain why these sentences have no grammatical counterparts with the clitic form of the pronoun, **Je me vous rappelle* and **Il se me rappelle* being ungrammatical.

there is no connection between the relative order of clitics and the existence of sentences with no grammatical outputs. But the devices that have been motivated to account for constraints on clitic order entail the possibility of sentences with no grammatical outputs. A linguistic theory that incorporates (90) posits the universality of surface structure constraints, which have been shown to be filtering devices, on clitic order. It therefore predicts that some sentences will be filtered out solely on the basis of clitic order, without regard for their properties in deep structure. (89) requires a notation in which more than one clitic can be assigned the same slot and which must be interpreted to mean that only one clitic from each slot is allowed. It follows that if any sentence requires two clitics that have been assigned the same slot in a surface structure constraint, it will have no grammatical realization in surface structure. A linguistic theory that incorporates (89) and (90) will thus predict the possibility of cases of syntactic blocking of exactly the kind observed. Such a theory can explain why the existence of constraints on clitic order in human languages entails the possibility of sentences with well-formed deep structures having no grammatical surface structures.

4.2. Evidence that the Constraint Cannot Be Stated by Phrase Structure Rules in the Base Component

Since the surface structure constraint (86) is of a form which is generable by a phrase structure rule, it might occur to someone to try to account for the order of clitics in Spanish by generating them in the order of (86) by means of a phrase structure rule in the base component, thereby dispensing with the need for a surface structure constraint. Any such attempt would immediately encounter insuperable difficulties. Only two of them will be pointed out here.

First, the clitics that occur with a given verb in surface structure are not necessarily generated with that verb in deep structure. This is so because clitic objects of lower verbs can move up to higher verbs. For example, the underlying structure which means "He wanted to continue shouting it to me" has three grammatical actualizations in surface structure:

> **(173)** a. Quería seguir gritándomelo.
> b. Quería seguírmelo gritando.
> c. Me lo quería seguir gritando.
> 'He wanted to continue shouting it to me.'

In (173a) the clitics *me* and *lo* are attached to the verb *gritando* 'shouting', whose objects they are in deep structure. In (173b), they have moved up to *seguir* 'continue'. In (173c) they are attached to *quería* 'he wanted'. As a result of the fact that the clitics in Spanish can move up to higher verbs, as illustrated in (173), the clitics that appear with a given verb in surface structure may have originated in deep structure either as objects of that verb or as objects of any of various embedded verbs. Using a phrase structure rule of the base to generate the clitics with the verb that they are attached to in surface structure would make it impossible to state strict subcategorizational and selectional facts about particular verbs, since these facts can only be stated in deep structure. It would also make it impossible to account for the distribution of the clitic pronouns. They may occur in surface structure with the verb with which they originate in deep structure, or they may move up to a higher verb, but they can not occur in both places at once. For example, it is necessary to generate the three sentences of (173), while ruling out as ungrammatical such nonsentences as

(174)   a. *Me lo quería seguir gritándomelo.
   b. *Me lo quería seguírmelo gritándomelo.

The attempt to position the clitics by means of a phrase structure rule in the base component seems quite hopeless.

This stratagem would still require the spurious *se* rule, since the motivations for this rule given in section 1 retain their validity. It would therefore be necessary to modify (86) slightly, and have the phrase structure rule introduce something like

(175)   (*se*)   (II)   (I) $\left(\underset{\text{Dat}}{\text{III}} \right)$ $\left(\underset{\text{Acc}}{\text{III}} \right)$

This modification is necessary in order to allow sequences of third person Dative and Accusative pronouns, since structures like

(176)   *Le lo di a Miguel.

must be generated. The spurious *se* rule will convert *(176) into the grammatical

(177)   Se lo di a Miguel.
   'I gave it to Miguel.'

Once this is done, however, it is necessary to postulate (86) as a surface structure constraint anyway, even if we try to generate the clitics in the correct order by a phrase structure rule whose right-hand side is (175). Since the grammar must generate

(178)   Pido que se me dé la razón, pero no *se me la* da.
   'I ask to be found right, but am not.'

there is nothing to prevent

(179)   *Pide que se le dé la razón, pero no *se le la* da.
   'He asks to be found right, but is not.'

which the spurious *se* rule will convert into

(180)   *Pide que se le dé la razón, pero no *se se la* da.

This sentence is ungrammatical, and a surface structure constraint is needed to rule it out. In similar fashion, since the grammar must generate

(181) Te le comiste el pan a Miguel, pero a mí no *te me lo* comas.
'You ate up Miguel's bread (on him), but don't you eat up mine (on me).'

it will also generate

(182) *Te me comiste el pan a mí, pero a Miguel no *te le lo* comas.
'You ate up my bread (on me), but don't you eat up Miguel's (on him).'

which the spurious *se* rule will convert into

(183) *Te me comiste el pan a mí, pero a Miguel no *te se lo* comas.

Similarly, there are grammatical sentences like

(184) No me le compliques la vida a mi chiquita.
'Don't complicate my little girl's life (on me).'

Use of the pronoun *la* instead of *la vida* results in an ungrammatical sentence

(185) *No me le la compliques.

which the spurious *se* rule will convert into

(186) *No *me se la* compliques.

which must be ruled out by a surface structure constraint. If we attempt to generate the clitics in their surface structure order in deep structure, (86) is still needed to rule out sentences like *(180), *(183), and *(186). The attempt to account for the order of the clitics by means of a phrase structure rule was based on the same false assumption that motivated the attempt to state the constraints on their order transformationally—the assumption that all that is needed is to get the clitics into the correct order. It has been seen that this assumption is false because it overlooks the essential aspect of the constraint—the filtering out of certain sentences as ungrammatical. This filtering function remains the strongest motivation for the surface structure constraint postulated here.

5. THEORETICAL CONSIDERATIONS

Evidence has been presented to show that the surface structure constraint (86) is part of the grammar of Spanish, and that the effect of this constraint cannot be obtained by means of transformations. It must be emphasized that a surface structure constraint like (86) differs from transformations in an essential way. An obligatory transformation must apply if its structural description is met, but there is no requirement that its structural description be met. A surface structure constraint like (86), on the other hand, requires that each clitic group in each sentence conform to it.

This chapter has not been concerned with the means by which the clitics get into the correct order so that the sentence in question can successfully negotiate the output constraint. There are two distinct tasks that must be accomplished by whatever grammatical devices are postulated to account for the facts of clitic placement. The first concerns the place in the sentence where the clitics must appear. The grammar of Spanish must somehow state that the clitics come before a finite verb, but after an infinitive, gerund, or imperative verb form, and that with past participles they must move up to the "auxiliary verb." [49] The second concerns the relative order of the clitics within the clitic group. This chapter has been concerned exclusively with the second problem, and only to the extent of showing that a surface structure constraint is necessary in the grammar. The existence of nonglobal constraints, such as those pointed out in section 3.6.1, shows that global surface structure constraints like (86) and (121) are not in themselves sufficient to account for all clitic phenomena in Spanish and French. The problems raised by nonglobal constraints and questions concerning the nature of the rules that move clitics to their final resting place in the sentence are left for future research.[50]

One might speculate about how the structures to which such clitic movement transformations apply should be identified. Two points deserve mention in this connection. First, linguistic theory must provide some means whereby transformations can refer to *clitics*. Since pronouns are NPs in underlying structure, it is beyond question that the clitic pronouns of Spanish are NPs in underlying representations. With respect to selectional and strict subcategorizational restrictions, as well as grammatical relations, all of which are stated in underlying structure, their status is exactly the same as that of other NPs. There is therefore no possible motivation for a node "Clitic" in underlying structure. Clitic movement transformations, however, move only clitics; other NPs are unaffected by these rules. Furthermore, it is just an accident of Spanish that all the clitics happen to be NPs. In the South Slavic languages, for example, the so-called "auxiliary verbs" are clitics as well, and undergo clitic movement transformations. It is therefore necessary for linguistic theory to provide the grammars of particular languages with a means of identifying certain lexical items as clitics and referring to them in rules. Second, once transformations can refer to clitics as such, it is no longer necessary for clitic movement transformations to be stated in terms of "structural descriptions" of the type that have been used in transformational grammars. That is, there is no need to specify the location in trees of the clitics that are to be moved. Direct and indirect objects, for example, could presumably be identified by their position in trees, but there is no point in doing this, since it is the fact that they are clitics rather than their location which makes them subject to movement.[51] What is

---

[49] The problem of stating the conditions under which clitics from a lower S can move up to the verb of a higher S is ignored here.

[50] For a detailed study of rules of clitic placement in French, see Kayne (1969). This work became available to me only after this chapter had been written.

[51] The constraints on movement discussed by Ross (1967) would automatically prevent movement of clitics across island boundaries.

needed is a way of specifying the domain of clitic movement transformations and stating that all clitics within that domain move to the verb.

The derived constituent structure produced by the rules that move clitics to the verb has not been discussed here. The question of whether there is a particular node in derived structure can be answered definitively only if there is a later transformation or transformations which must refer to that node. Since transformations of Spanish have not been investigated here, our discussion of this question will be brief, considering two possibilities and indicating what kinds of evidence could bear on the matter.

Consider first the question of whether there is a single node of some kind that dominates the entire group of clitic pronouns in surface structure. It is extremely doubtful that there is any such node. First, if such a node exists, it would have to be created in the course of the derivation, since the clitics originate in different parts of the sentence in underlying structure. The only transformations that could cause the creation of such a node are those that refer to clitics—that is, the transformation or transformations that move them to their final resting place in the sentence. In current transformational theory there is no way that such movement transformations could create a new node dominating the entire group of clitics. Second, such a node would yield highly unintuitive surface structures. Consider, for example, the sentence

(187)   Se me lo permitió.
'I was allowed (to do) it.'

Here we have the impersonal *se*, the indirect object pronoun *me*, and the direct object pronoun *lo*, which could be replacing a deleted sentence. What could a node dominating *se me lo* in surface structure be labelled? If there is no such node, there is no problem of what to label it. Third, it would be extremely difficult, if not impossible, to motivate such a node. To do this, it would be necessary to show that there is some transformation with respect to which the entire clitic group acts as a single constituent, in a way that cannot be accounted for in terms of the clitics acting individually. There may, in fact, be some rules with respect to which all the clitics in a given clitic group behave alike. For example, it is likely that this is the case with the rule of Spanish that under certain conditions moves all the clitics in a given clitic group to the verb of a higher S.[52] However, it would be difficult, if not impossible, to show that a node over the entire clitic group is needed to achieve this result. The rule in question may simply refer to clitics, which would all undergo it individually simply because they are all clitics. This is what happens with respect to the rule that moves the clitics to the verb in the first place. These three difficulties in establishing the existence of a node dominating the entire clitic group make it look extremely unlikely that such a node can be motivated.

---

[52] It is assumed here that there are at least two rules of clitic placement in Spanish—one that moves clitics to the verb in their S, and a later rule which, under certain conditions, moves the clitics to the verb of a higher S. Even if this assumption should prove to be incorrect, however, the argument would not be affected in an essential way.

A second possible derived constituent structure to consider is that which would be produced if the individual clitics are Chomsky-adjoined to the verb by the transformation which moves them there. If this is correct, and if all the clitic pronouns, including impersonal *se*, are dominated by NP, then the derived constituent structure of (187) would be roughly:

(188)

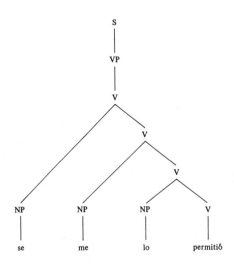

In order to motivate such a derived constituent structure, it would be neces-sary to show both that there are transformations that follow clitic placement with respect to which the clitics *se*, *me*, and *lo* act as NPs, and that there are later transformations with respect to which *lo permitió*, *me lo permitió*, and *se me lo permitió* act as verbs. Note that to show the former it would not be sufficient to show that the clitics *se*, *me*, and *lo* undergo some later rule. For example, if the initial rule of clitic placement is followed by another rule which under certain conditions moves the clitics up to a higher verb, this would not establish that clitics are dominated by NP in derived structure. This is because rules of clitic movement do not refer to *NPs*, but rather to *clitics*. I know of no evidence at present that is sufficient to motivate the derived structure sketched above, and hence the hypothesis that clitics are Chomsky-adjoined to the verb by the transformation which moves them.

Both the proposal that there is a node dominating the entire clitic group and the proposal that the clitics are Chomsky-adjoined to the verb impute a considerable amount of structure to the clitics-plus-verb group in derived structure. It is of course possible that evidence will be forthcoming to show that one of these proposals, or a similar one, is correct. In the absence of any such evidence, however, it seems that we do not need to attribute so much derived structure to the clitics-plus-verb group. Note that in (187) the only main stress in this sentence under normal intonation is on the verb *permitió.* The entire sentence is a single phonological word. It would therefore seem that the relevant generalization concerning the status of clitics in surface structure involves the fact that they form a single phonological word with the verb on which they lean. Their attachment to the verb would therefore be of a kind with other word-level phenomena in syntax. If this is correct, we would expect not to find evidence sufficient to motivate a richer derived structure.

Viewed in this light, the positioning of clitic pronouns in a fixed order adjacent to the verb in Spanish is quite similar to the situation in agglutinative languages, in which strings of morphemes that must come in a certain fixed order are attached to the verb. Parallels of this sort call into question the traditional division between morphology and syntax and suggest that some of the same grammatical devices may account for both syntactic and morphological phenomena.

What is striking about Spanish is the fact that the clitics are arranged in surface structure by *person,* and grammatical function plays no role whatever in determining their surface structure position. As a result, there are many sentences of Spanish in which the distinction between direct and indirect objects is not discernible in surface structure. Consider the following examples, cited by Heger (1966):

(189) a. Te me presento.
          'I introduce myself to you.'
      b. Te me presentas.
          'You introduce yourself to me.'

In (189a) *te* is Dative and *me* is Accusative, while in (189b) *me* is Dative and *te* is Accusative. The difference is that in (189a) the verb is first person singular, while in (189b) it is second person singular. But with certain other verbs, we find just the reverse. For example, consider

(190) a. Te me imagino caminando en la nieve.
          'I imagine you (to myself) walking in the snow.'
      b. Te me imaginas caminando en la nieve.
          'You imagine me (to yourself) walking in the snow.'

In (190a), in which the verb is first person singular, *me* is Dative and *te* is Accusative, while in (190b), in which the verb is second person singular, *te* is Dative and *me* is Accusative. And if the verb of (189) is put in the third person, we get an ambiguous sentence:

(191) Te me presenta.
      'He introduces me to you; He introduces you to me.'

Whatever the exact derived constituent structure in these five sentences may be, it is clear that the distinction between direct and indirect objects is in no way overtly marked in surface structure.[53]

---

[53] These examples show once again that grammatical relations are not always marked in surface structure, and that it is therefore necessary to have a deeper level of representa-

The surface structure constraints that we have postulated to account for clitic order in Spanish and French are reminiscent of the "morpheme order charts" to be found in the linguistic literature, as well as the "decade notation" used in *IJAL* and other publications, especially in the late forties and the fifties.[54] Morpheme order charts usually list morphemes in columnar charts similar to (86), and they are usually accompanied by a statement to the effect that only one item from each column may be chosen and that they must come in the order in which the columns are represented in the chart. The "decade notation" assigns the decade 10 to the class of affixes which can not be separated from the stem (or base, or theme, and so on), and individual affixes in the class are numbered 11, 12, 13, and so on. The class of affixes which can be separated from the stem only by members of 10 is assigned to decade 20, and its members are numbered 21, 22, 23, and so on. A decade in this notation corresponds to a column of a chart in the notation of (86).

In the light of the proposal that the notation of (86) will capture genuine generalizations in surface structure constraints on clitics in all languages, it is of course not surprising that equivalent notations should have been used by earlier researchers in the field. It would be surprising if this were *not* the case. Yet, the theoretical proposals and conclusions of this paper differ from earlier work in three respects. First, the theoretical apparatus used has been justified on the basis of empirical evidence. Second, it has been shown that charts in the notation of (86) perform a *filtering function* in grammars. Third, I have attempted to extract from (86) what is universal and incorporate it into universal grammar. These differences are a consequence of the fact that this work has proceeded from two central concerns—that of constructing a portion of an explicit grammar of Spanish capable of making correct predictions about speakers' intuitions about novel sentences, and that of constructing an explicit theory of linguistic

---

tion at which grammatical relations are represented. Furthermore, if the rules that move clitics to the verb say only that clitics move to the verb, without specifying the origin of the clitics in the sentence, then the clitic movement transformations are not "reversible." A theory of performance, which must be concerned with the question of how the speaker uses his internalized grammar in speaking and understanding, cannot simply say that the listener "reverses the transformations" to arrive at the underlying structure on the basis of the surface string he hears, since clitic movement transformations may be irreversible. This may also be true of the scrambling rules we find in so-called "free word order" languages. This should not, of course, come as a great surprise. There is no reason to believe that transformations should be "reversible," and that the listener "reverses" them in decoding a sentence, just as there is no reason to believe that the transformations involved in the generation of a given sentence are actually performed by the speaker in the course of uttering it.

54 For examples of morpheme order charts, see Hymes (1955), Li (1946, 409–419), and Whorf (1946, 384). An equivalent type of statement in terms of "positions" is given by Hockett (1948). The decade notation seems to have been introduced by C. F. Voegelin. As examples of the decade notation, see Bergsland (1951) and Garvin (1948). This list of references is, of course, by no means exhaustive or even representative. I am indebted to Fred W. Householder, Jr., for acquainting me with the decade notation and some of the literature cited here.

universals capable of making correct predictions about "novel" languages.

Morpheme order charts and the decade notation seem to have been regarded as useful devices for the taxonomic description of surface structures. As soon as one thinks in terms of a generative theory, however, it becomes unclear how these devices are to be interpreted. For example, if (86) is taken to be a morpheme order chart in the traditional sense, it would most likely be interpreted as an instruction to arrange the clitics of Spanish in the order it illustrates. But as has been seen in section 4, a grammar that attempts to account for Spanish clitic order in this way is inadequate; it can not account for the ungrammaticality of sentences like *(39), *(46b), *(51b), *(62b), *(160), *(161), and *(164). The crucial point about (86) is that it performs a *filtering function,* filtering out sentences with sequences of clitics that do not conform to it. And the notion "filtering function" simply has no meaning outside a generative theory, since without such a theory there is nothing to filter. The discovery that these devices do have a filtering function and that there are semantically well-formed sentences that have no grammatical realization due to constraints on clitic order is thus a consequence of the attempt to construct explicit grammars which relate underlying and surface structures.

There is also a difference in orientation between this paper and earlier studies that used similar notational devices. It is the difference between classification of data and a theory. If one is concerned solely with classification of data, it does not matter what kinds of devices one uses; one is as good as another, and it is perfectly all right to switch from one to another at will. A linguistic theory such as I have been attempting to construct here, however, is quite different. It states that in an adequate grammar the notation of (86) *must* be used to construct surface structure constraints on clitic order. This requirement embodies the prediction that the use of this notation will make it possible to state global constraints on clitics in additional languages—that the generalizations that emerge from data on clitics in other languages will be the kinds of generalizations that can be stated in this notation. This theory is therefore subject to empirical test. The kinds of evidence that would show (89) to be incorrect have already been pointed out. Within the framework of a universal theory of this kind, facts that cannot be stated in this notation and generalizations that cannot be captured by it become important because they put the theory itself into question. They cannot be treated in an ad hoc manner,[55] but must be studied further

---

[55] As long as morpheme order charts and the decade notation were used merely for convenience in classifying data and did not embody any empirical predictions, data that could not readily be handled by them had no theoretical significance and seems not even to have occasioned much comment. For example, Bergsland (1951, 172) states that "forms with 210, 220 may behave syntactically like forms with 110, 120, but are also frequent before, in Eskimo also after, noun-like forms in phrases with number and case agreement, while noun-like forms in Aleut seem to combine in attribute + head phrases only." Also from Bergsland: "The alternate *-q . . . marks absolutive case in final position, but may in Eskimo, at least partly, precede 180 and 122 + 170, 180" (p. 168). "112–113 may follow 130, 140 and precede 170 and 122 + 170, — 112–113

to determine their consequences for the theory. What I have been attempting to do, then, is to take morpheme order charts and decade notation and incorporate them into a universal linguistic theory as filtering devices that apply to the output of the transformational component.[56]

+ 180 and in Eskimo also $112 + 122 + 180$" (p. 168). It is not at all clear whether or not any of these facts have any bearing on the universals proposed here. The literature may contain real counterexamples to them. Anyone who can point this out and show how linguistic theory must be modified to accommodate them will be making a significant contribution to theory.

[56] The notation of (86) also bears a certain superficial resemblance to the kinds of devices that are posited in tagmemic theory. Before attempting to assess the consequences of our findings on Spanish for tagmemic theory, however, it would be well to point out that it is not at all clear whether or not tagmemics *is* a theory in any clear sense. It certainly provides a means of organizing linguistic data and can be used as a guide in doing field work. But that does not make it a theory. A substantive theory of language makes concrete claims and predictions about language, specifying the kinds of facts that can and can not be found in human language. If one finds facts which the theory predicts can not occur, or fails to find the kinds of facts that it predicts do occur, then the theory is shown to be incorrect and must be revised or abandoned. In brief, a substantive theory is subject to empirical test and refutation. In this chapter I have attempted to show that the theory of language of Chomsky (1965) is inadequate because it does not include surface structure constraints, and I have proposed a modification of the theory along these lines. If tagmemics is not just a way of organizing linguistic data, but is rather a substantive theory of language that makes claims about the nature of linguistic reality, then it is subject to empirical test and refutation in exactly the same way.

The basic concept of tagmemics is the "tagmeme," which Elson and Pickett (1964, 57) define as follows:

The tagmeme, as a grammatical unit, is *the correlation of a grammatical function or slot with a class of mutually substitutable items occurring in that slot. This slot-class correlation has a distribution within the grammatical hierarchy of a language.*

The term *slot* refers to the grammatical function of the tagmeme. The terms "subject," "object," "predicate," "modifier," and the like indicate such grammatical functions.

A common misunderstanding of the term tagmeme is that the term slot is taken to refer exclusively or primarily to the linear position in which morphemes and morpheme sequences are found. This is not the case. Slot refers primarily to grammatical function and only secondarily to linear position.

To the extent that tagmemics is a substantive theory of language, then, it claims that the sentences of human languages can be represented in terms of "tagmemes"—slots which represent grammatical functions. If tagmemics is to be a substantive theory, it must define and constrain the notion "grammatical function." If new "grammatical functions" can be invented ad hoc for each new language one encounters, then the basic claim of tagmemics is empty and it fails to make any substantive predictions about human languages. The quotation from Elson and Pickett suggests that the notion "grammatical function" is to be interpreted in a rather traditional way pending development of a theory that explicitly specifies the possible "grammatical functions" to be found in human languages.

Although the "tagmemic formulas" used in the literature on tagmemics produce models of sentences that bear some resemblance to (86), the basic claim of tagmemics is that these slots represent grammatical function. Our findings on object pronouns in Spanish therefore constitute counterevidence to the basic claim of tagmemics. The "slots" into which the mutually substitutable classes of Spanish clitic pronouns must

In this chapter, the terms "surface structure constraint" and "output condition" have been used interchangeably; the precise level of derivations at which these constraints apply has not been specified. In Spanish, the constraint must apply after the spurious *se* rule, which is a very late, low-level rule. Furthermore, there do not seem to be any syntactic rules in Spanish that must apply after (86). It therefore seems that (86) applies to the final output of the syntactic component.

It is not clear at present whether or not linguistic theory must allow transformations to apply after the application of a surface constraint on clitics. Spanish provides no evidence that this is necessary. The evidence from French, as was noted in footnote 35, is rather inconclusive. If there are any languages for which it can be shown that some other rule must follow the application of the surface constraint on clitics, then linguistic theory must provide for this eventuality. This would immediately raise certain questions concerning (90). If there is no limit to the number or type of transformations that can apply after a surface constraint on clitics, then (90) would be weakened considerably. However, the fact that it is difficult to find clear cases of rules applying after a surface constraint on clitics suggests that if any such rules exist, there are severe limitations on what they may be. It would then be necessary to determine whether or not there is a significant linguistic level slightly deeper than surface struc-

---

go do not represent *function* at all, but rather *person*. In a theory which postulates an underlying structure distinct from surface structure, grammatical relations can be represented in underlying structure. The fact that they are not overtly marked in surface structure in Spanish therefore does not constitute a problem for the theory. Because tagmemic theory attempts to state grammatical relations in terms of tagmemes defined on surface structures, however, it can either attempt to account for grammatical relations and ignore the constraints on clitic order and co-occurrence in surface structure, or it can account for the latter and ignore the former. An adequate theory of language, of course, must account for both.

The only published treatment of Spanish within a tagmemic framework that I have seen is that of Brend (1968). Brend chooses to set up tagmemes in terms of grammatical function, postulating a "phrase indirect object" tagmeme and a "phrase object" tagmeme as part of the "transitive predicate." Since tagmemics operates at a single level, which is essentially that of surface structure, the fact that Brend defines these tagmemes in terms of direct and indirect object leaves her with no way of stating clitic order and co-occurrence restrictions in Spanish, since these are based not on direct versus indirect object, but rather on person. In Brend's analysis, fillers of the phrase indirect object tagmeme are *me, te, le, nos, les,* and spurious *se.* Fillers of the phrase object tagmeme are *me, te, le, lo, la, nos, las, los,* and reflexive *se.* Brend's analysis allows any filler of the indirect object tagmeme to be followed by any filler of the direct object tagmeme. It thus incorrectly predicts that sentences with the clitic sequences **me te, *me nos, *me se, *me me, *te se, *te te, *le me, *le te, *le nos, *le se, *nos me, *nos te, *nos nos, *nos se *les me, *les te, *les nos,* and **les se* are grammatical. Furthermore, Brend's grammar does not account for any of the sequences of more than two clitics that *are* grammatical. The essential point is not that Brend's grammar is inadequate, but rather that these inadequacies are inevitable within the tagmemic framework once one decides to state the direct and indirect object relations on surface structure in Spanish. Had Brend chosen instead to set up tagmemes on the basis of the order of pronominal objects in surface structure, she would not have been able to state the grammatical relations of direct and indirect object in a satisfactory way.

ture [57] at which these constraints apply. At present, I know of no evidence which bears on these issues.

6. SUMMARY

In this chapter, I have attempted to show, first, that the chart notation of (86) captures genuine generalizations and therefore has a place in linguistic theory. Second, I have attempted to show that constraints expressed in this notation perform a filtering function, discarding any sentence generated by the transformational component that does not conform to them. The argument in both instances was based on data drawn from Spanish. I then went on to formulate universals from which the grammatical devices found to be necessary in the grammar of Spanish would follow automatically. It was shown that these proposed universals explain additional facts of Spanish, as well as a number of facts of French. The third and most important goal of this chapter, then, has been to show that facts which in the absence of any kind of universal linguistic theory are bizarre become completely regular when viewed in the light of a universal theory that predicts what kinds of generalizations can emerge from linguistic data. Such a theory is able not only to account for the observed facts, but also to explain them.

---

[57] A linguistic level of this sort, called "shallow structure," has been suggested by Paul Postal.

3 SURFACE STRUCTURE CONSTRAINTS AND PHONOLOGICAL INFORMATION

The theory of generative grammar has generally maintained a position that can be formulated roughly as follows:

> **(1)** Phonological properties of formatives have no relevance for syntax.

A position that follows from (1) is:

> **(2)** The syntactic component of grammars does not refer to phonological information.

(1) and (2) are not axioms, but empirical hypotheses. Their truth or falsehood can only be determined on the basis of empirical data drawn from natural languages.

A theory that denied (2), for example, would be making empirical claims about human language very different from those made by the current theory of generative grammar. Such a theory would allow grammars to include syntactic transformations like the following:

> **(3)** a. A verb moves to sentence-initial position if it contains a liquid.
> b. A count noun moves to pre-article position in the noun phrase if its first segment is a stop.
> c. An adjective is placed after the head noun if its inflectional ending is phonologically zero.

It is an empirical question whether languages have rules like those in (3). At present, there seems to be no evidence to indicate that they do.

It is the purpose of this chapter to show that while (2) is probably true, (1) is not. In particular, I wish to show that a theory of language which includes surface structure constraints of the kind motivated in Chapter Two makes one very specific prediction about the role of phonological information in syntax, and that examples of exactly the predicted type are to be found in human languages.

In Spanish, all clitics with the phonological shape *se* behave alike with respect to the surface structure constraint (86) discussed in Chapter Two, regardless of their syntactic origin. It follows that (86) applies at a stage of derivations at which morphemes have already been given phonological shape.

A second property of (86) is the fact that it is sensitive only to what actually appears in surface structure. It was shown in Chapter Two that whereas

(4)   Te me escapaste.
'You escaped from me.'

is perfectly grammatical, the corresponding underlying structure which would mean "I escaped from you" has no grammatical realization for many speakers of Spanish.

(5)   a. *Te me escapé.
b. *Me te escapé.

Yet, this deep structure is well-formed, for it is an underlying constituent of the grammatical sentence

(6)   Me le escapé a Jorge, pero a ti no.
'I escaped from Jorge, but not from you.'

From these facts the conclusion was drawn in Chapter Two that (86) rejects as ungrammatical only strings violating it that actually appear in surface structure.

A theory of language which allows the surface structure constraint (86), then, posits the existence of a kind of well-formedness condition that applies at a stage of derivations after morphemes have been given phonological shape and filters out sentences in which violations of the well-formedness condition are audible in surface structure. Such a theory of language therefore predicts that even if the syntactic component of grammars can make no reference whatever to phonological information, one aspect of the phonological shape of morphemes can have syntactic consequences. A surface structure constraint could impose a template of the form

(7)   A   B   C

on a particular grammatical construction. (7) would filter out as ungrammatical any string in which another morpheme D intervenes between A and B or between B and C. Suppose, however, that the morpheme D intervenes between B and C, but D happens to be phonologically zero. Since (7) will apply after morphemes have been given phonological shape, and since it is sensitive only to what is actually audible in surface structure, it follows that (7) will filter out any sentence in which the D intervening between B and C is phonologically constituted, but it will not notice anything wrong with those strings in which D happens to be phonologically zero. As a result, examples in which D is phonologically zero will qualify as grammatical, while in all cases in which it is phonologically constituted, the sentence will be filtered out as ungrammatical. In this way, a theory of language that includes surface structure constraints like (86) and does not allow syntactic rules and constraints to make direct reference to phonological information makes a very specific prediction about the role of phonological shape in grammaticality:

(8) There can be cases in which a sentence will be grammatical if a particular morpheme is phonologically zero and ungrammatical otherwise.

It remains to see whether (8) is correct. In this chapter, I wish to present two examples of the type that (8) predicts will occur in human languages.

The first example of this type was discovered by Kenneth Hale in his study of Walbiri, a language spoken in central Australia. In Walbiri, clitics occur in second position in the sentence, after the first constituent. The clitic which marks present tense is *ka,* and the Nominative, Accusative, and Dative clitics for the first, second, and third person singular are as follows:

	Nom.	*Acc.*	*Dat.*
I Sg.	ṇa	t^{y}u	t^{y}u
II Sg.	npa	ŋku	ŋku
III Sg.	φ	φ	ḷa

A clitic copy of each Nominative, Accusative, or Dative noun phrase in the sentence must obligatorily occur in second position.[1] The clitics are subject to the following surface structure constraint, expressed in the notation of (86) of Chapter Two:

(9)   Tense   Nom   Dat/Acc   ḷa   t^{y}inta

Although the clitics ḷa and t^{y}inta are of interest to a more detailed study of Walbiri syntax (cf. Hale [1967]), they are not directly relevant to the topic of this chapter, and so they will be ignored in what follows.

A few sentences of Walbiri will illustrate how things work.

(10)   ŋat^{y}ulu-ḷu   ka-ṇa-ŋku   n^{y}a-n^{y}i   n^{y}untu
       I   Erg   see-Pres   you
       'I see you.'

---

[1] Walbiri is an Ergative language, with noun phrases marked for Ergative (subject of a transitive verb), Absolutive (subject of an intransitive verb or object of a transitive verb), or Dative case. The fact that in clitics case works on a Nominative-Accusative system, rather than an Ergative-Absolutive system, suggests that case in full noun phrases is also on a Nominative-Accusative system at the stage of derivations at which noun phrases are doubled as clitics, and that the Ergative-Absolutive system found in full noun phrases in surface structure is a phenomenon restricted to late stages of derivations.

(11) nʸuntulu-ḷu   ka-npa-tʸu   nʸa-nʸi   ŋatʸu
you   Erg   see-Pres me
'You see me.'

(12) ŋatʸulu-ḷu   ka-ṇa-φ   nʸa-nʸi   kaḷi
I   Erg   see-Pres boomerang
'I see the boomerang.'

In each of these examples, the clitic complex follows the first constituent in the sentence. (10) has the present tense marker *ka,* the first person singular Nominative clitic *ṇa,* and the second person singular Accusative clitic *ŋku.* (10) is actually somewhat artificial, for a Walbiri would naturally delete the subject and object in this example and say simply

(13) nʸa-nʸi   ka-ṇa-ŋku
'I see you.'

(11) could similarly be reduced to

(14) nʸa-nʸi   ka-npa-tʸu
'You see me.'

and (12) to

(15) kaḷi   ka-ṇa-φ   nʸa-nʸi
'I see the boomerang.'

Word order is quite free in Walbiri, at least in simple sentences. To make the examples easier to follow, however, I will give only the variants of sentences in which the deletions illustrated by (13–15) have not taken place, and I will not vary the word order as a Walbiri might do. Although the resulting sentences would therefore sound somewhat artificial to a Walbiri, they will hopefully make the exposition somewhat easier to follow for those readers who do not speak Walbiri.

The crucial point about Walbiri that is of relevance here is this: the Dative and Accusative clitics óccupy the same column of (9).[2] The universal notation in which (9) is expressed, motivated in Chapter Two, thus predicts that a Dative and Accusative clitic cannot co-occur in the same clitic group. And this is correct. Sentences with the verb *punta* 'take', which takes both Dative and Accusative objects, illustrate the point. One cannot say in Walbiri

(16) *nʸanuŋu-ḷu   ka-φ-ŋku-tʸu   punta-ṇi   nʸuntu   ŋatʸu-ku
he   Erg   take-Pres you   me   Dat
'He is taking you from me.'

or

(17) *nʸanuŋu-ḷu   ka-φ-tʸu-ŋku   punta-ṇi   ŋatʸu   nʸuntu-ku
he   Erg   take-Pres me   you   Dat
'He is taking me from you.'

_____
[2] As was noted above, the third person singular Dative clitic *ḷa* is systematically ignored throughout the discussion.

The ungrammaticality of *(16) and *(17) is due to the clitic sequences *ŋku-tʸu* and *tʸu-ŋku*. Any sentence which contains both of these clitics in the same clitic group will be filtered out as ungrammatical by (9).

An important generalization emerges from additional data from Walbiri:

(18) Although a Dative and Accusative clitic cannot co-occur in the same clitic group in Walbiri, this is possible just in case the Accusative clitic is phonologically zero.[3]

Since the third person singular Accusative clitic is phonologically zero in Walbiri, a Dative and Accusative noun phrase can co-occur in the same simple sentence in Walbiri if the Accusative is third person singular. Thus, the following sentences are fully grammatical:

(19) nʸanuŋu-ḷu ka-ϕ-ϕ-tʸu punta-ṇi kaḷi ŋatʸu-ku
　　　he　　　Erg　　　　　　take-Pres boom. me　Dat
　　　'He is taking the boomerang from me.'

(20) nʸanuŋu-ḷu ka-ϕ-ϕ-ŋku punta-ṇi kaḷi nʸuntu-ku
　　　he　　　Erg　　　　　　take-Pres boom. you　Dat
　　　'He is taking the boomerang from you.'

(21) ŋatʸulu-ḷu ka-ṇa-ϕ-ŋku punta-ṇi nʸanuŋu nʸuntu-ku
　　　I　　　Erg　　　　　　take-Pres him　　you　Dat
　　　'I am taking him from you.'

The fact that simple sentences of Walbiri that contain both a Dative and an Accusative noun phrase are grammatical just in case the Accusative clitic is phonologically zero is a striking illustration of the situation that (8) states will occur in human languages.

One might attempt to invalidate this example by arguing that the relevant constraint in Walbiri is not (18) but rather:

(22) Although a Dative and Accusative clitic cannot co-occur in the same clitic group in Walbiri, this is possible just in case one of the two clitics is third person singular Accusative.

(22) would account for the data given so far, and is not an illustration of the situation that (8) states will occur.

It is possible to show that (18) is correct and (22) incorrect by considering Walbiri examples in which the Accusative noun phrase is plural. The third person plural clitic for both Dative and Accusative is *tʸana*.

(23) ŋatʸulu-ḷu ka-ṇa-tʸana nʸa-nʸi kaḷi-patu
　　　I　　　Erg　　　　　see-Pres boomerang-plural
　　　'I see the boomerangs.'

If the Accusative noun phrase is Inanimate, as it is in (23), it is possible to use ϕ instead of *tʸana* as the Accusative clitic. A variant of (23), then, is

---

3 There are no Dative clitics in Walbiri that are phonologically zero.

(24)   ŋat^{y}ulu-ḷu   ka-ṇa-φ   n^{y}a-n^{y}i   kaḷi-patu
'I see the boomerangs.'

Now, of the two ways one might try to say "He is taking the boomerangs from me" in Walbiri, only one is grammatical.

(25)   a.   *n^{y}anuŋu-ḷu   ka-φ-t^{y}ana-t^{y}u   punta-ṇi   kaḷi   ŋat^{y}u-ku
he   Erg   take-Pres   boom.   me   Dat
b.   n^{y}anuŋu-ḷu   ka-φ-φ-t^{y}u   punta-ṇi   kaḷi   ŋat^{y}u-ku
he   Erg   take-Pres   boom.   me   Dat
'He is taking the boomerangs from me.'

It is the same with the sentence "He is taking the boomerangs from you."

(26)   a.   *n^{y}anuŋu-ḷu   ka-φ-t^{y}ana-ŋku   punta-ṇi   kaḷi
he   Erg   take-Pres   boom.
n^{y}untu-ku
you   Dat
b.   n^{y}anuŋu-ḷu   ka-φ-φ-ŋku   punta-ṇi   kaḷi   n^{y}untu-ku
he   Erg   take-Pres   boom. you   Dat
'He is taking the boomerangs from you.'

If *t^{y}ana* is used for the third person plural Accusative, the sentence is ungrammatical, for it contains both a Dative and an Accusative clitic. But if the phonologically zero variant of the Accusative is used, the sentence qualifies as grammatical. If the third person plural Accusative noun phrase is Animate, the *t^{y}ana* clitic *must* be used; in this case, zero is not a possible alternative. As a result, one cannot say "He is taking the children from you" in Walbiri.

(27)   a.   *n^{y}anuŋu-ḷu   ka-φ-t^{y}ana-ŋku   punta-ṇi   kuḍu-patu
he   Erg   take-Pres   child-plural
n^{y}untu-ku
you   Dat
b.   *n^{y}anuŋu-ḷu   ka-φ-φ-ŋku   punta-ṇi   kuḍu-patu
he   Erg   take-Pres   child-pl
n^{y}untu-ku
you   Dat

*(27a) is ungrammatical because (9) filters out sentences with the clitic sequence *Acc Dat* (in this case, *t^{y}ana ŋku*), and *(27b) is ungrammatical because φ cannot be used for an Animate object. The examples in (25–27) show that (22) is incorrect. If (22) is to account for these examples, it would have to be changed to something like

(28)   Although a Dative or Accusative clitic cannot co-occur in the same clitic group in Walbiri, this is possible just in case one of the two clitics is third person singular Accusative or the phonologically zero variant of the third person plural Accusative.

But now it is clear that (28) misses the generalization which (18) states.[4]

Finally, it can be shown that the phenomena in question are indeed due to the surface structure constraint (9) on the order of clitics. While it is impossible to say "He is taking the children from you" in Walbiri (cf. *(27)), the deep structure underlying this sentence must be well formed, for it also underlies the embedded sentence in

(29) ŋatʸulu-ḷu ɸ-ṇa-ɸ nʸanuŋu nʸa-ŋu, nʸuntu-ku
I Erg him see-Past you Dat
kuḍu-patu punta-ṇinʸtʸa-kura
child-pl take-Gerund-Complementizer
'I saw him take the children from you.'

which is fully grammatical. A complement sentence embedded with the *kura* complementizer does not contain clitics agreeing with noun phrases in the complement. As a result, the output does not run afoul of (9), and a grammatical sentence results. Similarly, while it is impossible to say "He is taking you from me" and "He is taking me from you" in Walbiri (cf. *(16) and *(17)), if these sentences are embedded in *kura*-complements in which there are no clitics, the result is perfectly grammatical.

(30) kuḍu-patu-ḷu ɸ-lu-ɸ-ɸ nʸanuŋu nʸa-ŋu, ŋatʸu-ku
child-pl-Erg him see-Past me Dat
nʸuntu punta-ṇinʸtʸa-kura
you take-Gerund-Complementizer
'The children saw him take you from me.'

(31) kuḍu-patu-ḷu ɸ-lu-ɸ-ɸ nʸanuŋu nʸa-ŋu, nʸuntu-ku
child-pl-Erg him see-Past you Dat
ŋatʸu punta-ṇinʸtʸa-kura
me take-Gerund-Complementizer
'The children saw him take me from you.'

The ungrammaticality of the sentences with both a Dative and a phonologically constituted (nonzero) Accusative clitic must therefore be due to the surface structure constraint (9).

In the absence of a theory of surface structure constraints, one might easily conclude that these examples from Walbiri show that the syntactic component of grammars must be able to make reference to the phonological shape of morphemes in order to state the generalization (18). But a theory that gave the syntactic component this power would thereby make it possible for the syntax to include rules like those in (3) and would therefore fail to account for the nonoccurrence of such rules in human languages.

One might try to dispute the validity of the generalization (18) in

---

[4] Essentially the same argument can be based on the dual in Walbiri, since the Accusative dual clitic for Inanimate objects can optionally be zero. An Accusative dual noun phrase can co-occur with a Dative noun phrase in the same simple sentence just in case the phonologically zero variant of the Accusative dual clitic is used.

Walbiri by arguing that what it means for a clitic to be phonologically zero is for it just not to be there. To argue that phonologically zero clitics simply are not present seems reasonable enough as far as surface structure is concerned, and the fact that surface structure constraints are not sensitive to them could be taken as supporting evidence. But there is no doubt that these clitics, even those which may not be there in surface structure, are present at earlier stages of derivations. Consider the alternative. It was mentioned above that all Nominative, Accusative, and Dative noun phrases are obligatorily doubled as pronominal clitics, which are moved to second position. Obviously, the most general formulation of this doubling rule would simply refer to Nominative, Accusative, and Dative noun phrases, without regard for their person or number. In order to maintain that in those cases where the clitics are phonologically zero no doubling takes place, it would be necessary to place the following conditions on the application of the doubling rule:

(32) a. Clitic doubling is obligatory for all first and second person noun phrases, for all Dative third person noun phrases, for all Animate Accusative third person dual and plural noun phrases, and for all Nominative third person dual and plural noun phrases.
      b. Clitic doubling is optional for Inanimate Accusative third person dual and plural noun phrases.
      c. Clitic doubling does not apply to Accusative and Nominative third person singular noun phrases.[5]

In other words, conditions on the clitic doubling transformation such as (32) could be used to express the fact that Accusative and Nominative third person singular clitics are always phonologically zero, and Inanimate Accusative third person dual and plural clitics can optionally be phonologically zero. But since the phonological shape of *all* clitics must be indicated somewhere in the grammar anyway, it is pointless to give the list of just those clitics whose phonological shape is zero in the form of a set of conditions on the clitic doubling rule.[6] One might feel driven to such a maneuver if it were the only means of avoiding a syntactic transformation or constraint which referred directly to phonological information, for to allow that would be to allow rules like those in (3), which do not occur in human languages. But we have seen that the treatment of phonologically zero clitics by (9) in Walbiri follows automatically from the theory of surface structure constraints developed in Chapter Two on the basis of evidence from Spanish. Conditions on clitic doubling in Walbiri such as (32)

---

[5] It might be possible to eliminate (32a) by stating (32b) and (32c) and saying that clitic doubling is obligatory in all other cases. This could be done if "all other cases" could be defined in such a way as to exclude objects of postpositions. But even so, the argument against (32) given here would retain its validity.

[6] In the Epilogue, it is proposed that conditions on transformations like those in (32) be ruled out in principle.

are therefore not necessary to avoid direct reference to phonological information in syntax. The generalization (18) causes no difficulties and requires no power to be given to grammars in addition to what they have already been shown to need on independent grounds.

In the absence of a theory of surface structure constraints, the generalization (18) in Walbiri might be taken to indicate that it is necessary for the syntax to refer directly to phonological information, with all the excessive power that that would entail. But a theory of language that includes surface structure constraints of the kind motivated in Chapter Two automatically predicts that generalizations like (18) will emerge from data in human languages. (18) in Walbiri thus provides strong support for the theory.

Another example of a generalization of the same type occurs in English, in the *go Verb* construction studied by Lee Linthicum. Consider the following paradigm:

(33) a. I go study Greek.
      b. You go study Greek.
      c. *He goes study Greek; *He goes studies Greek.
      d. We go study Greek.
      e. They go study Greek.

This *go Verb* construction which lacks the infinitival *to* between *go* and the verb is grammatical everywhere but in the third person singular. It would seem that the grammar contains a constraint like:

(34) The *go Verb* construction is ungrammatical if the subject is third person singular.

However, the question which corresponds to *(33c) is perfectly grammatical:

(35) Does he go study Greek?

This shows that (34) is incorrect, and we must look elsewhere for the correct generalization.

On the basis of the evidence presented so far, the following generalization suggests itself:

(36) The *go Verb* construction is grammatical if the ending on *go* is phonologically zero; it is ungrammatical if *go* has a phonologically constituted ending.

(36) accounts for the grammaticality of all the sentences in (33) except *(33c), and for the seemingly mysterious fact that (35), the question corresponding to *(33c), is grammatical. Significantly, (36) is exactly the kind of generalization which the theory of surface structure constraints developed here predicts will be found in human languages.

Testing to see whether (36) is the correct generalization, we note that it accounts for the fact that the *go Verb* construction is grammatical in imperatives

(37)   Go study Greek.

with modals

(38)   a. He will go study Greek.
b. He may go study Greek.
c. He must go study Greek.

and in the infinitive.

(39)   He wants to go study Greek.

It correctly accounts for the contrast in grammaticality between

(40)   He likes to go study Greek.

and

(41)   *He likes going study Greek.

All of these facts follow from (36).

The significance of (36) lies in the fact that it is the type of generalization which follows automatically from the notation for the statement of surface structure constraints developed in Chapter Two. The constraint on the *go Verb* construction can be stated as follows:

(42)   Output condition on the *go Verb* construction: *go* Verb

(42) is to be interpreted as a template which applies to the output of the transformational component in the same way that (86) and (114) of Chapter Two and (9) of this chapter do.[7] (42) will correctly filter out as ungrammatical all strings in this construction in which something intervenes between *go* and the verb. Sentences in which *go* has an ending, such as *-s* or *-ing,* will be filtered out as ungrammatical. But in sentences where the ending happens to be phonologically zero, (42) will see nothing between *go* and the verb, and the sentence will qualify as grammatical.

Although (42) was established on the basis of the fact that only phonologically zero endings are possible on *go* in the *go Verb* construction, it makes additional predictions. It correctly predicts that a verb-particle construction is not possible with *go*

---

[7] Note that in order for (42) to apply correctly to sentences, there must be some way of identifying the *go Verb* construction in surface structure. This is completely analogous to the problem of how the constraint (86) on clitics in Spanish discussed in Chapter Two applies to sentences. There must be some way of identifying clitic sequences in sentences, for if (86) were applied to some other part of sentences, the sentences in question would be filtered out as ungrammatical because they contain material other than the permitted *se II I III.*

For most speakers of English the verb *come* can also be used in the *go Verb* construction. A more adequate version of (42) should therefore give the disjunction $\left\{ {go \atop come} \right\}$ instead of just *go.*

(43)   a.   *Go over study Greek.
       b.   *Go in study Greek.

but only with the second verb in the construction

(44)   a.   Go talk over your problems with someone.
       b.   Go look up the information.

since in *(43), but not in (44), the particle intervenes between *go* and
the verb. (42) also predicts correctly that adverbs cannot intervene between *go* and the verb

(45)   a.   *Go at once confer with the manager.
       b.   *Go immediately confer with the manager.

but are possible after the verb

(46)   a.   Go confer at once with the manager.
       b.   Go confer immediately with the manager.

The correctness of these predictions provides further support for the theory,
which was developed on the basis of totally different data.

I have not attempted to show here that the constraint on the *go Verb*
construction cannot be stated transformationally, because it is the transformational solution that must bear the burden of proof. Since the role
of phonological zeroes in the *go Verb* construction is exactly what follows
from the nature of surface structure constraints, treating the *go Verb*
construction as a surface structure constraint does not increase the power
of grammars in any way. To state the constraint transformationally would
make it necessary to make the transformational component sensitive to
the phonological shape of verb endings in English, thereby allowing rules
like those in (3) in the syntax and increasing the power of the syntactic
component far beyond what seems to be necessary. That the syntax does
not have such power is of course not true a priori. But the burden of proof
is on anyone who would claim that it does.

It has been the purpose of this chapter to show that it is possible for
the phonological shape of morphemes to have syntactic consequences
without the syntactic component actually making direct reference to phonological information. I have discussed only examples in which grammaticality depends on whether a particular morpheme is phonologically
zero or phonologically constituted. I have attempted to show that in these
cases the syntactic consequences of the phonological shape of morphemes
is exactly what is predicted by a theory that does *not* allow the syntactic
component to refer directly to phonological information. Of course, it
cannot be said with certainty that no evidence will ever be forthcoming
which shows that the syntactic component must refer to phonological information. It should be borne in mind, however, that any theory allowing
that will thereby allow rules like those in (3), which seem not to occur in
human languages. The best policy, then, when examples arise that seem

to indicate that the syntactic component must refer to phonological information, would be very much like that adopted here. First determine the limits on which phonological properties of formatives have syntactic consequences and exactly what their syntactic consequences are, and then seek to develop a theory which does *not* allow direct reference to phonological information in the syntax but from which the phonological properties in question will have the observed syntactic consequences. If this kind of research deepens our insight into the kinds of devices that grammars contain, this discussion of how the syntactic role of phonological zeroes follows from the nature of surface structure constraints will have been instructive.

4 A TYPOLOGICAL DIFFERENCE AMONG LANGUAGES

In French, one may question any object or adverbial constituent of a subordinate clause introduced by *que*.

(1) a. Qui a-t-il dit que Martin avait envie de voir?
        'Who did he say that Martin felt like seeing?'
     b. À qui a-t-il dit que Nicole a donné l'argent?
        'Who did he say that Nicole gave the money to?'
     c. Où a-t-il dit que Roger irait prendre sa retraite?
        'Where did he say that Roger would go to retire?'
     d. Quand a-t-il dit que les flics viendraient?
        'When did he say that the cops would come?'

However, it is impossible to question the *subject* of such a subordinate clause.

(2) *Qui a-t-il dit que s'est évanoui?
        'Who did he say (that) fainted?'
(3) *Qu'a-t-il dit que s'est passé?
        'What did he say (that) happened?'
(4) *Qui a-t-il dit que va venir ce soir?
        'Who did he say (that) is going to come tonight?'

The same thing happens under relativization. It is possible to relativize any object or adverbial constituent in such subordinate clauses, but not the subject.

(5) a. la speakerine qu'il a dit que Martin avait envie de voir
        'the announcer that he said (that) Martin felt like seeing'
     b. la personne à qui il a dit que Nicole a donné l'argent
        'the person who he said (that) Nicole gave the money to'
     c. le pays où il a dit que Roger irait prendre sa retraite
        'the country where he said (that) Roger would go to retire'

(6)   *la speakerine qu'il a dit que s'est évanouie
      'the announcer that he said (that) fainted'
(7)   *les événements qu'il a dit que se sont déroulés
      'the events which he said (that) took place'
(8)   *la personne qu'il a dit que va venir ce soir
      'the person that he said (that) is going to come tonight'

It would appear at first glance that it is necessary to impose a special constraint on movement transformations such as Question Formation and Relativization in French to prevent them from moving the subject, and only the subject, out of subordinate clauses introduced by *que*. I will here propose a different solution—that the grammar of French contains the following surface constraint:

(9)   Any sentence other than an Imperative in which there is an S that does not contain a subject in surface structure is ungrammatical.

This constraint applies to examples like (6) in the following way. Before the application of the relativization transformation, the structure underlying (6) looks something like this:

(10)

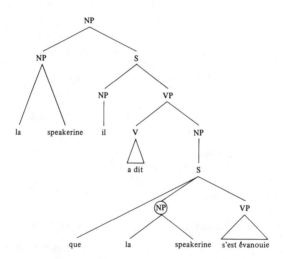

The relativization rule pronominalizes *la speakerine,* the circled NP in (10), and moves it to the front of the relative clause,[1] producing a derived structure like:

---

[1] The precise details of relativization are not relevant here. The important point is that the noun phrase in the relative clause that is identical to the antecedent is taken out of its position in the relative clause and is moved to the front of the relative clause, where it ends up as a relative pronoun—*qui* or *que.*

(11)

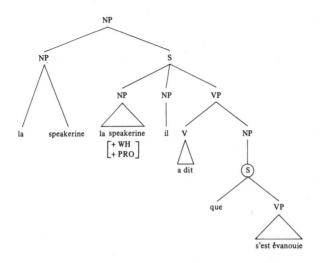

When the surface structure constraint (9) applies, the embedded (circled) sentence in the relative clause has no subject, and the sentence is discarded as ungrammatical. In examples like those in (5), on the other hand, it is not the subject of an embedded sentence that is moved to the front of the relative clause. When the constraint (9) is applied, there is a subject in each S in the tree. These examples therefore qualify as grammatical.[2]

---

2 In relative clauses in which the subject has been relativized, the relative pronoun satisfies the requirement that each S contain a subject in surface structure. In

  (i) l'homme qui va venir ce soir
       'the man who is going to come tonight'

for example, the derived structure is something like

  (ii)

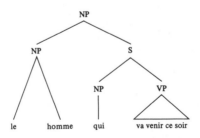

The relative pronoun *qui* acts as subject in surface structure, and as a result, (ii) is not rejected as ungrammatical by (9).

For some speakers of French, the structure underlying *(11) would be actualized as

The surface structure constraint (9) therefore accounts for the fact that sentences like *(2–4) and *(6–8), in which an embedded subject has been relativized or questioned, are ungrammatical, while sentences like (1) and (5), in which some constituent other than the subject has been relativized or questioned, are fully grammatical. It does this without making it necessary to place ad hoc constraints on the Relativization and Question Formation transformations in order to prevent the subject—and only the subject —of a subordinate clause from undergoing these rules.

The surface structure constraint (9) also accounts for another fact of French that without (9) would be a completely unrelated phenomenon. This is the fact that subject pronouns in French cannot be deleted. It is often said that those languages which allow deletion of subject pronouns allow it because they have sufficient inflection to make the deleted subject recoverable. This is often true in French, yet the resulting sentences are ungrammatical.

> **(12)**   a.   *Avons travaillé toute la journée.
> '(We) worked all day long.'
> b.   *Êtes parti trop tôt, il paraît.
> '(You) left too early, it seems.'
> c.   *Ont mangé la soupe sans cuillère.
> '(They) ate the soup without a spoon.'

And other languages allow deletion of subject pronouns even where ambiguity results. In Italian, for example, we find

> **(13)**   Sono qui.
> 'I am here; They are here.'

The fact that subject pronouns in French can not be deleted cannot be explained by a theory that claims that this happens only where there is sufficient inflection to prevent ambiguity. This fact can be explained, however, by the constraint (9).

This hypothesis entails the claim that the ungrammaticality of sentences like *(2–4) and *(6–8), on the one hand, and the ungrammaticality of sentences like those in *(12), on the other, are different aspects of the same phenomenon; it is claimed that all of these sentences are rejected as ungrammatical by the surface structure constraint (9). Now let us put this

---

> (iii)   la speakerine qu'il a dit qui s'est évanouie
> the announcer that he said who fainted
> 'the announcer that he said fainted'

Similarly, the structure underlying *(2) would be realized as

> (iv)   Qui a-t-il dit qui s'est évanoui?
> who did he say who fainted
> 'Who did he say fainted?'

It is not clear how the relative pronoun *qui* gets into the position after *dit* in these sentences. Given that it is there, however, it follows from the fact that (9) does not filter out (ii) that it will not filter out (iii) or (iv) either.

theory to the crucial test. If it is correct, it should be the case that in languages which allow deletion of subject pronouns—languages in which sentences like *(12) are grammatical—sentences like *(2–4) and *(6–8) will be grammatical as well.[3] I will use Spanish as an example of such a language, since in Spanish sentences like *(12) without subject pronouns are grammatical:

(14)   Hemos trabajado todo el día.
'(We) have worked all day.'

And the prediction is borne out: in Spanish it is possible to question or relativize the subject of an embedded sentence.

(15)   ¿Quién dijiste que salió temprano?
'Who did you say (that) left early?'
(16)   ¿Qué dijiste que pasó?
'What did you say (that) happened?'
(17)   el tipo que dijiste que salió temprano
'the guy that you said (that) left early'
(18)   las cosas que dijiste que pasaron
'the things that you said (that) happened'

We now have a hypothesis according to which French differs from Spanish in that the grammar of French has the surface structure constraint (9), while the grammar of Spanish has no such constraint. This constraint simultaneously accounts for two otherwise separate facts—the deletability of subject pronouns and the ability to question or relativize the subject of an embedded sentence—by means of a single constraint.

This surface structure constraint not only accounts for the correlation between the ability to question or relativize the subject of an embedded sentence and the deletability of subject pronouns, it also accounts for a wide range of other phenomena which represent systematic differences between French and Spanish. The constraint (9) makes the claim that no nonimperative sentence of French is grammatical unless it has a subject in surface structure. It therefore explains *why* it is that French has an expletive subject in a wide range of different constructions. Spanish, on the other hand, has no surface structure constraint that requires the presence of a subject in surface structure, and it does not have expletive subjects.

The expletive *il* in French appears in a wide range of different constructions.[4] In each case, there is no corresponding surface structure subject in Spanish. I list below some of the constructions in which this systematic difference between the two languages can be seen.

---

[3] I expect this to be the case if it is possible to question or relativize noun phrases in subordinate clauses in the first place. In Russian, for example, it is impossible to question or relativize anything at all in subordinate clauses of the type under discussion, so we cannot expect the subjects of such subordinate clauses to be questionable or relativizable.

[4] The question of whether dummy subjects like French *il* are present in deep structure or introduced by transformations is not directly relevant to the hypothesis. This matter is discussed briefly in what follows.

In sentences with weather verbs, *il* occurs as surface structure subject in French.

(19) Il pleut.
'It's raining.'

(20) Il fait beau temps.
'It's nice weather out.'

In Spanish, the verb appears without any surface structure subject.

(21) Llueve.
'It's raining.'

(22) Hace buen tiempo.
'It's nice weather out.'

No surface structure subject is possible with these expressions in Spanish.

(23) a. *Él llueve.
b. *Ello llueve.

In French, the expletive *il* appears in sentences which have an extraposed sentential subject.

(24) Il est évident que l'impérialisme suédois est à bout de souffle.
'It is clear that Swedish imperialism is on its last legs.'

In Spanish, such sentences have no subject in surface structure.

(25) Es evidente que no pasarán.
'It is clear that they won't get through.'

We find the same thing in expressions of time, in which French again uses expletive *il* as a dummy subject in surface structure.

(26) Il est tard.
'It's late.'

The corresponding Spanish sentence has no surface structure subject at all.

(27) Es tarde.
'It's late.'

(26) would be ungrammatical without a surface structure subject, while (27) would be ungrammatical if a dummy pronoun were put in.

It might be argued that these facts can be accounted for simply by postulating a transformation in French that introduces the dummy subject *il* in sentences that lack a subject late in derivations. Such a proposal would be unable to account for the full range of facts presented here, however, for two reasons. First, the dummy subject in French is not always *il,* but is sometimes *ce.*

(28) C'est beau les montagnes.
'Mountains are beautiful.'

(29)   C'est étonnant le nombre de gens qui mangent à l'américaine.
'It's amazing the number of people who eat American style.'

Assuming that the distribution of *il* and *ce* can be stated transformationally, it would require at least two transformations to insert the appropriate dummy subjects. Second, and much more important, transformations that introduce dummy subjects into sentences that lack a subject in surface structure cannot also account for the fact that subject pronouns can not be deleted in French, or the fact that the subject of a subordinate clause can not be questioned or relativized. It is the correlation of these three sets of facts that is explained by the surface structure constraint (9).

The question of whether the dummy subjects *il* and *ce* in French are transformationally introduced or present in deep structure will be left open here, since it is not directly relevant to our hypothesis. Let us consider each of these two possibilities in turn, and determine the status of our hypothesis in each case.

If the dummy subjects are present in deep structure, our hypothesis explains why they cannot be deleted in French, in exactly the same way that it explains why subject pronouns cannot be deleted in French.

If, on the other hand, the dummy subjects are not present in deep structure, but rather are transformationally introduced, our hypothesis explains why French has transformations that introduce such dummy subjects into surface structures. It does this in the following way. There are sentences—(19), (20), and (26), for example—for which there is no evidence of the presence of any subject at all in deep structure. In such languages as Spanish, which lack the constraint (9), there is no evidence for such sentences' having a subject at *any* stage of derivations. There are other sentences, such as (24), that have no subject once the Extraposition transformation has applied. This is so because, since we are now assuming that the dummy subjects are not present in deep structure, the deep structure of (24) looks like

(30)

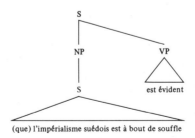

(que) l'impérialisme suédois est à bout de souffle

Since the Extraposition transformation moves a subject S to the end of the sentence, the application of Extraposition produces a derived constituent structure like

(31)

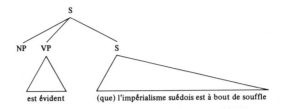

in which there is no subject. Now, if the grammar of French includes the surface structure constraint (9), sentences like (19), (20), (24), and (26) will be ruled out as ungrammatical, *unless* the grammar also contains transformations that insert dummy subjects into these sentences prior to the application of the constraint (9). The presence of (9) in the grammar of French does not *require* that the grammar contain rules to provide sentences like (19), (20), (24), and (26) with dummy subjects. It does entail, however, that if the grammar does not have any such rules, there will be no way to actualize the deep structures of any of these sentences grammatically. Our hypothesis does not predict that this situation can not arise. It predicts only that if sentences of this type are grammatical in a language for which the surface structure constraint (9) is motivated on independent grounds, then such sentences will have dummy subjects in surface structure.

The form of explanation here is somewhat different from that which is generally found in the literature on generative grammar. Our hypothesis does not explain why certain sentences are grammatical, but rather why grammatical sentences contain subjects in surface structure in French— that is, why grammatical sentences have the form that they do. The surface structure constraint (9) is an explanatory hypothesis that explains *why* it is that in French there are sentences with dummy subjects, subject pronouns cannot be deleted, and the subjects of subordinate clauses can not be questioned or relativized. It explains why we find these facts, rather than others, by means of the requirement that in French each S must have a subject in surface structure.

As a result, the explanatory power of this hypothesis extends beyond the domain of expletive subjects like *il* and *ce* in French. It also explains why an underlying Pro subject [5] is spelled out *as a subject* in surface structure in French. We are referring to the formative *on,* which is a subject in surface structure. It occurs in subject position in sentences like

(32)   On veut que la Nouvelle Angleterre soit libre et indépendante.
    'Pro wants New England to be free and independent.'

---

[5] By "Pro" I do not mean any pronoun, but rather the entity that is the underlying subject of the Spanish sentences with "impersonal *se*" discussed in Chapter Two, and which is spelled out as *on* in French and *man* in German.

and it behaves like a subject in that it inverts with the verb in questions.

(33) Veut-on que la Nouvelle Angleterre soit libre et indépendante?
'Does Pro want New England to be free and independent?'

In Spanish, on the other hand, an underlying Pro subject is spelled out as impersonal *se*. As was seen in Chapter Two, impersonal *se* behaves like an object pronoun in surface structure, positioning itself next to the verb with the other object pronouns.

(34) Se quiere que la Nueva Inglaterra sea libre y independiente.
'Pro wants New England to be free and independent.'

(35) Se te permitió dormir toda la mañana.
'Pro allowed you to sleep all morning'; that is, 'You were allowed to sleep all morning.'

As a result, Spanish sentences like (34) and (35), which have a Pro subject in deep structure, have no subject at all in surface structure. The fact that sentences like (32) have a surface structure subject in French, while the Spanish counterpart (34) lacks a surface structure subject, is another manifestation of the systematic difference between French and Spanish that is under discussion here. This difference is explained by our hypothesis, according to which the grammar of French has the surface structure constraint (9), while the grammar of Spanish does not.

It follows from the nature of this hypothesis that it makes claims about French but not about Spanish. Since it postulates the constraint (9) in the grammar of French, the existence of grammatical sentences in French other than imperatives that lack a surface structure subject would make it necessary to modify or abandon (9). By the same token, it is only for French that the hypothesis has any explanatory power, since nothing whatsoever is being said about a language such as Spanish that does not have the constraint (9) in its grammar. A language that has no such surface structure constraint *could,* for example, have a transformation which introduces expletive subjects in various sentences, but, lacking the constraint (9), there is no reason for it to have such a rule. The fact is that most languages which have no such surface structure constraint also have no expletive subjects in surface structure.

It seems that a large number of languages are like Spanish in that they have no constraint like (9) in their grammars. They therefore allow questioning and relativization of the subject of a subordinate clause,[6] they allow deletion of subject pronouns,[7] and they generally lack expletive subjects

---

[6] If they allow anything to be moved out of subordinate clauses, as was noted in Footnote 3.

[7] The conditions under which subject pronouns can be deleted vary within certain limits in different languages, but that is not relevant here. The issue here concerns languages in which subject pronouns *can* be deleted, regardless of the conditions under which this takes place.

in surface structure. The languages in this category include Italian, Serbo-Croatian, Arabic, Hebrew, Hausa, Walbiri, and Basque.[8]

It is more difficult to find languages that, like French, have the constraint (9) in their grammars. In some cases it is more difficult to establish whether there is motivation for (9) in a particular language. English, for example, has the same restriction as French on relativization or questioning of the subject of a subordinate clause introduced by *that*. It is possible to question any constituent of such subordinate clauses except the subject.

(36) a. What did he say that Laura bought?
      b. Where did he say that Laura bought the rutabaga?
      c. When did he say that Laura bought the rutabaga?

(37) *Who did he say that bought the rutabaga?
(38) *What did he say that happened?

It is the same with relativization.

(39) a. the rutabaga that he said that Laura bought
      b. the place where he said that Laura bought the rutabaga
      c. the day that he said that Laura bought the rutabaga

(40) *the woman that he said that bought the rutabaga
(41) *the events that he said that happened

But whereas there is no way to make sentences like *(37), *(38), *(40), and *(41) grammatical in French, they are grammatical in English if the complementizer *that* is deleted.

(42) Who did he say bought the rutabaga?
(43) What did he say happened?
(44) the woman that he said bought the rutabaga
(45) the events that he said happened

The question before us is how these facts in English are to be accounted for. Does the grammar of English include the surface structure constraint (9), or can these facts be explained in some other way?

One alternative would be to order the *that*-deletion rule to follow Relativization and Question Formation and to place a condition on it such that although it is an optional rule, it is obligatory if *that* is immediately followed by a VP. The *that*-deletion transformation would then relate pairs of sentences such as

(46) a. He said that no one would ever find him.
      b. He said no one would ever find him.

by means of its optionality. But if the subject of an embedded sentence had been removed by Relativization or Question Formation, *that*-deletion

---

8 I am indebted to Wayles Browne for this information on Serbo-Croatian, Michael Brame on Arabic, John Ritter on Hausa, Kenneth Hale on Walbiri, and Rudolf de Rijk on Basque.

would be obligatory, and *(37), *(38), *(40), and *(41) would be converted into the grammatical (42), (43), (44), and (45), respectively.

Another possibility would be to say that there are two rules that delete the complementizer *that*. One would be an optional rule and would relate pairs of sentences like (46a) and (46b). The other rule would apply not only to *that*, but to all complementizers in English, and would obligatorily delete any complementizer that is immediately followed by a VP. This rule would purport to express a generalization to the effect that complementizers do not occur before a VP in English. As a result, *(37), *(38), *(40), and *(41) would, by this means as well, emerge as the grammatical sentences (42), (43), (44), and (45), respectively.

What these two proposals have in common is that they find some way of getting grammatical sentences out of *(37), *(38), *(40), and *(41). We can show that they are both wrong by finding examples where the *that* simply can not be deleted. This is the case with the verb *allow*, as can be seen in:

(47)   a.   Clyde allowed that Henrietta likes spumoni.
        b.   *Clyde allowed Henrietta likes spumoni.

With *allow*, as in the examples we have already considered, a grammatical sentence results if any constituent of the subordinate clause other than the subject is questioned.

(48)   What did Clyde allow that Henrietta likes?
(49)   *Who did Clyde allow that likes spumoni?

If the counterproposals outlined above were correct, the following sentence would be grammatical.

(50)   *Who did Clyde allow likes spumoni?

It is the same with relative clauses. We may relativize anything but the subject of the subordinate clause.

(51)   the kind of spumoni that Clyde allowed that Henrietta likes
(52)   *the girl that Clyde allowed that likes spumoni

If the counterproposals above were correct, the following example would be grammatical.

(53)   *the girl that Clyde allowed likes spumoni

Since neither *(50) nor *(53) is grammatical, the counterproposals above are incorrect. It is not the case that the complementizer *that* is obligatorily deleted before a VP. We must now be able to rule out as ungrammatical not only *(37), *(38), *(40), and *(41), but also *(49) and *(52). The surface structure constraint (9) does just that. I conclude that this surface structure constraint is part of the grammar of English.

A similar example which shows that this constraint is needed in the grammar of English is provided by sentences like

(54)   a.   It must be the case that Clarita robs churches.
b.   *It must be the case Clarita robs churches.

Since *that* can not be deleted after *the case,* it is possible to construct a similar argument for (9) based on sentences with *the case.* Any constituent of the embedded sentence except the subject can be questioned or relativized.

(55)   What must it be the case that Clarita robs?
(56)   *Who must it be the case that robs churches?

If *that*-deletion were obligatory, as the two counterproposals above would have it, the following sentence would be grammatical:

(57)   *Who must it be the case robs churches?

Since it is not, the counterproposals above are incorrect, and the surface structure constraint (9) must be included in the grammar of English.

There may be some variation from one speaker to another with regard to the deletability of *that* with *allow* and *the case.* All that is needed to motivate (9) for a given dialect is to find a verb or expression that allows questioning and relativization from subordinate clauses embedded beneath it, and that does not allow deletion of *that* after it. The argument is then as given above for *allow* and *the case.*

Now that the surface structure constraint (9) has been included in the grammar of English, it can be seen that it automatically accounts for what would otherwise be a mysterious limitation on movement of constituents out of *in order for* clauses. For example, consider a sentence like

(58)   Sarah worked for six months in order for that man to be able to buy a car.

A noun phrase in object position in the *in order for* clause can be questioned or relativized, as in

(59)   the car that Sarah worked for six months in order for that man to be able to buy

But a noun phrase in subject position can not be questioned or relativized.

(60)   *the man that Sarah worked for six months in order for to be able to buy a car

Since the *in order for* clause contains a full sentence (although the verb is in infinitival form), there is no reason for it not to be dominated by an S-node. In the case of *(60), then, the subject has been moved out of the clause, leaving an S in surface structure that does not contain a subject. The constraint (9) therefore rejects it as ungrammatical. In the case of (59), on the other hand, it is the object that is moved, (9) is not violated, and the result is grammatical. The constraint (9) thus accounts for the difference in grammaticality between (59) and *(60). Note also that if the counterproposal discussed above were correct, and complementizers were obligatorily deleted before a VP in English, thereby accounting for the grammaticality of (42–45), then the complementizer *for* in *(60) should be deleted, and the result should be grammatical. But it is not:

(61) *the man that Sarah worked for six months in order to be able to buy a car.

This counterproposal cannot account for examples like these, while the surface structure constraint (9) does.

One might attempt to account for the ungrammaticality of the examples under discussion by means of a transformational constraint that would cause the derivation to block if the subject of an embedded S is moved out of it by Question Formation or Relativization. This is essentially the course taken by Ross (1969b, 296) in proposing the following restriction on relative clause formation in English:

> An NP which is the subject of an embedded S (that is, an NP which is directly dominated by a node *S* other than the topmost node *S*) may not be relativized (i.e. moved to the front of the sentence) unless it is the first constituent of the sentence of which it is the subject.

In order for clauses make it possible to show in a particularly clear way that the ungrammaticality of examples like *(60) is due to a surface structure constraint rather than to a transformational constraint. A transformational constraint to account for the ungrammaticality of such examples would cause the derivation to block if the subject is moved out of an S. It would therefore be impossible for the application of any later transformations to make the output grammatical. If, on the other hand, the ungrammaticality of *(60) and other examples of the type discussed in this chapter is due to a surface structure constraint, the only thing that is relevant is whether or not each S in the surface structure contains a subject. A transformation that deletes an embedded S after the subject has been moved out of it would provide us with a crucial test between these two alternatives.

The rule of Sluicing motivated by Ross (1969a) is just the kind of rule that is needed for the crucial test.[9] Sluicing converts structures like

(62) Marge is head over heels in love with someone, but I don't know who Marge is head over heels in love with.

into structures like

(63) Marge is head over heels in love with someone, but I don't know who.

Ross shows that Sluicing applies after Question Formation has moved the *wh*-word to clause-initial position in the embedded question in the second conjunct. There are, therefore, derivations in which Question Formation first moves the subject out of an embedded S, and then the rest of the embedded S is deleted by the Sluicing transformation. One such example, at the stage of derivations after the application of Question Formation, is

---

9 I am indebted to Michael Szamosi for pointing this out to me.

(64) *Sarah worked for six months in order for someone to be able to buy a car, but I don't know who Sarah worked for six months in order (for) to be able to buy a car.

If the ungrammaticality of *(60) is due to a transformational constraint, subsequent application of Sluicing will make no difference; the derivation is blocked once and for all at the stage at which *(64) is produced. If, on the other hand, *(60) is ungrammatical because of a surface structure constraint, subsequent application of Sluicing can produce a grammatical sentence. And it does:

(65)   Sarah worked for six months in order for someone to be able to buy a car, but I don't know who.

I conclude that the ungrammaticality of examples like *(60) is indeed due to a surface structure constraint, as stated in (9).

With (9) in the grammar of English, ungrammatical sentences such as *(37), *(38), *(40), *(41), *(49), *(52), and *(60) are correctly rejected as ungrammatical. However, the sentences (42–45) must not be ruled out by (9) as ungrammatical, since they are perfectly grammatical. In order to account for these examples, we must assume that when *that* is deleted, the S-node above the embedded sentence is pruned away.[10] Then, when the surface structure constraint checks each S in the tree to make sure that it has a subject, there will be no S-node above the embedded sentence, and it will consequently not be rejected as ungrammatical. The derived constituent structure of *(40), then, would look something like this:

(66)

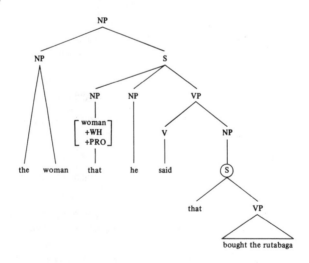

---

[10] A theory of tree-pruning is proposed and discussed in Ross (1967b), Chapter Three, and Ross (1969b). Since the former proposal was written more recently than the latter, that is the one on which my discussion of pruning is based.

that has not been deleted, and the S-node that is circled consequently remains above the embedded sentence. The surface structure constraint (9) finds that this tree contains an S which lacks a subject in surface structure, and consequently rejects it as ungrammatical. If *that* has been deleted, on the other hand, this S-node is pruned away and the derived constituent structure looks something like this: [11]

(67)

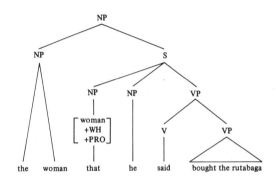

The tree contains no S's that lack a subject, and it is consequently not rejected as ungrammatical by (9). Aside from the necessity of accounting for the difference in grammaticality between sentences like *(40) and those like (44), I have no other evidence that deletion of *that* causes pruning.

Ross (1967b) proposes a general condition according to which pruning of S-nodes occurs whenever an S-node does not branch, that is, whenever it dominates only one constituent. The examples given in support of this are cases where what begins as an entire embedded sentence in deep structure ends up as just a single constituent in surface structure. This is the case when a relative clause is reduced to just an adjective, and when a full sentence is reduced to just a noun phrase by Comparative Reduction, to produce sentences like

(68)   Joe is faster than Pete.

I am proposing here that *that*-deletion also causes pruning, converting (66) to (67).

One might attempt to preserve Ross's condition that only S-nodes that do not branch are pruned, noting that in (66) it is only because of the presence of *that* that the S-node continues to branch; as soon as *that* is deleted, the circled S-node no longer branches, and it is consequently pruned. If this is correct, *that*-deletion does not cause pruning by itself; it is only when the deletion of *that* results in an S-node that does not branch

---

11 I have also pruned away the NP-node that dominates the circled S-node in (66), as seems correct. However, I know of no general principle that predicts that this NP-node must be pruned.

that pruning takes place. However, as Arlene Berman has pointed out to me, this proposal does not work. Under the assumption that sentence adverbs such as *probably* are immediately dominated by the S-node in surface structure, the presence of such an adverb will cause the S-node to continue to branch, even if *that* is deleted. If the attempt to preserve Ross's condition is correct, pruning will not take place, and it will be impossible to question or relativize the subject of an embedding with a sentence adverb, even if *that* has been deleted. However, this is not the case.

> **(69)**   a.   Who does Bill think probably jimmied the lock?
>   b.   the man who Bill thinks probably jimmied the lock

In order for these examples not to be rejected as ungrammatical by (9), it is necessary that the S-node above the embedded sentence be pruned. Since the S-node in question continues to branch, it is necessary to maintain that *that*-deletion causes pruning independently of the condition for pruning proposed by Ross. This hypothesis accounts for the grammaticality of (42–45) and (69). It also entails that in the paradigm

> **(70)**   a.   It is obvious that the electorate is gullible.
>   b.   It is obvious the electorate is gullible.
>   c.   The candidates know that the electorate is gullible.
>   d.   The candidates know the electorate is gullible.

in (70a) and (70c), but not in (70b) and (70d), there is an S-node above the complement in surface structure. This may be correct, but I have no direct evidence to support it.[12] At any rate, it is clear that if the hypothesis proposed here is correct, deletion of the *that* complementizer in sentences like (42–45) and (69) must cause pruning of the S-node above the embedded sentence prior to the application of the surface structure constraint (9).

Now that (9) has been motivated for English, it provides an *explanation* for other phenomena in English, as was the case in French. It ex-

---

[12] The fact that Extraposition has applied in (70b) is not evidence that there is an S-node above *the electorate is gullible* in surface structure. This is because *that* can not be deleted when the sentence has not been extraposed. Thus we have *That Claude came late annoyed me,* but not **Claude came late annoyed me.* This means that *that*-deletion does not occur until after Extraposition has applied. If *that*-deletion causes pruning of the dominating S-node, then, this will not occur until after Extraposition has applied. The fact that Extraposition has applied therefore tells us nothing about whether we have an embedded S-node in surface structure.

     Reflexivization also fails to provide any evidence as to where pruning takes place. Ross (1967b) proposes that Equi-NP Deletion causes pruning of the embedded S-node in sentences like *Dan forced Carol to photograph him.* If this is correct, pruning of the embedded S-node must take place after Reflexivization has applied for the last time, in order to prevent the ungrammatical **Dan forced Carol to photograph himself.* Similarly, the fact that we get *Dan thinks Carol photographed him* rather than **Dan thinks Carol photographed himself* fails to provide us with any evidence as to whether the embedded clause in such sentences is dominated by an S-node in surface structure, since pruning could occur after Reflexivization has applied for the last time, as in the sentences with *force* above.

plains why subject pronouns can not be deleted in English, although there are many instances in which the verb is sufficiently inflected to make the result completely unambiguous.[13]

(71) *Am making good progress.

(72) *Is spending the summer in Vermont.

(73) *Tries to please his mother-in-law.

Surface structure constraint (9) also provides an explanation for the various dummy subjects in grammatical English sentences.

(74) *It* is raining.

(75) *It* is conceivable that electoral politics could be a vehicle for effecting social change.

(76) *It* is five o'clock.

(77) *It's* me.

(78) *There* is a daffodil under the pillow.

Leaving open the question of whether these dummy subjects are present in deep structure or transformationally introduced,[14] the surface structure constraint (9) is an explanatory hypothesis that explains why all grammatical English sentences have some kind of subject in surface structure— that is, why they have the form that they do.

I will refer to languages such as French and English, which have the surface structure constraint (9) in their grammars, as Type A languages. Languages that do not have this surface structure constraint I will call Type B languages. These include Spanish, Italian, Serbo-Croatian, Arabic, Hebrew, Hausa, Walbiri, and Basque. Given this definition of Type A and Type B languages, every language must be either of one type or the other.

I have been careful to characterize languages as Type A only if the surface structure constraint (9) is needed in their grammars to reject as ungrammatical any sentences in which the subject of a subordinate clause has been relativized or questioned. Since my hypothesis makes no claims about Type B languages, which do not have the constraint (9), it would not be disconfirmed if there were a Type B language in which subject pronouns can not be deleted and which has expletive subjects like French *il* and English *it* and *there*. Under my hypothesis, these facts would be

---

[13] Sentences of this sort are acceptable as telegraphic or headline style, which suggests that in this style the constraint (9) is not operative.

[14] In the case of *there,* there are strong arguments that it is transformationally introduced, as argued in Footnote 6 of Perlmutter (1970). It is also clear that not all instances of expletive *it* can originate from the phrase structure rule NP → (Det) N (S) posited by Rosenbaum (1967). Under Rosenbaum's analysis, the *it* is introduced as the *N* in the above structure, and shows up when the subject S is extraposed, as in *It is obvious that time is short.* Rosenbaum's analysis therefore cannot account for examples that have expletive *it* but no extraposed sentence. But there are such cases, for example: *It's amazing the number of people who eat American style; It's neat the way that works.* These examples suggest that English has a transformation which inserts expletive *it* into sentences which lack a subject at some late stage of derivations.

accidental in a Type B language, whereas they are necessary and therefore explained in a Type A language. It seems that Dutch is just such a language. In Dutch, such a sentence as

(79) Wie vertelde je, dat gekommen was?
'Who did you say (that) had come?'

in which the subject of a subordinate clause introduced by *dat* 'that' has been moved away by Question Formation, is perfectly grammatical. On the basis of the grammaticality of (79), Dutch must be classified as a Type B language. Now it happens that in Dutch subject pronouns can not be deleted, and the language has the expletive subjects *het* and *er* that function much like *it* and *there* in English. Under my hypothesis, these facts of Dutch are accidental. It is of course possible that these facts of Dutch are not accidental and could be captured by a theory superior to the one proposed here, just as it is also possible that they *are* accidental and therefore predictable by no general theory. For the present, since there is no theory that predicts that Dutch *must* exhibit these facts, they remain accidental facts and therefore are fundamentally different from the analogous facts in French and English, for which my hypothesis predicts that, given the ungrammaticality of sentences in which the subject of a subordinate clause has been removed, the language *must* have expletive subjects and cannot have deletion of subject pronouns. Whereas these facts in French and English are explained by my hypothesis, the same facts in Dutch are not.

If my hypothesis is correct, it provides a way of determining whether or not the subject of an embedded S in deep structure continues to be dominated by the embedded S-node in surface structure in Type A languages. If it can not be questioned or relativized, while other constituents of the embedded S *can* be questioned or relativized, it must still be the subject of the embedded S in surface structure. If, on the other hand, it *can* be questioned or relativized, it must occupy a position in surface structure in which it is no longer the subject of an S.

Consider a dialect of English that, like my own, exhibits the following paradigms:

(80) a. I hate it for Lucille to sing Dixie.
b. I hate for Lucille to sing Dixie.
c. *I hate Lucille to sing Dixie.
(81) a. *I expect it for Lucille to sing Dixie.
b. *I expect for Lucille to sing Dixie.
c. I expect Lucille to sing Dixie.

A deep structure for these sentences like the one proposed by Rosenbaum (1967) would be:

(82)

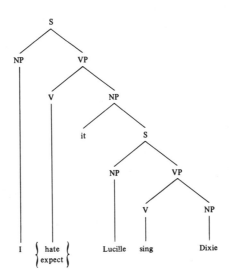

With the verb *expect,* the subject of the embedded sentence undergoes It-Replacement, being substituted for the *it* dominated by the NP that immediately dominates the embedded S, while the rest of the embedded S is brought under the domination of the matrix VP. This results in a derived structure like

(83)

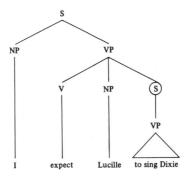

At this point, Ross's theory of pruning predicts that the embedded (circled) S-node in (83) will be pruned, since it dominates only one constituent. Pruning of the embedded S-node produces the derived structure

(84)

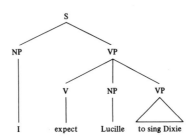

The crucial aspect of this derived structure is that *Lucille* is now the object of *expect* in the matrix sentence.

With *hate,* on the other hand, It-Replacement does not apply, with the result that *Lucille* remains in the embedded sentence in a derived structure that is essentially the same as the deep structure (82).

(85)

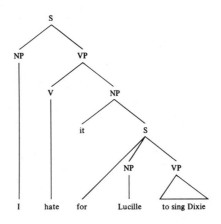

According to Ross's theory of pruning, the embedded S-node in (85) will *not* be pruned, since it dominates more than one constituent. An optional rule deletes the *it* in sentences with *hate,* thereby producing (80b) from the structure which underlies (80a).

This analysis accounts for the inability of *it* to occur in object position with *expect* and a complement sentence by means of a rule that substitutes the subject of the embedded sentence for this *it*. With *hate* the *it* can occur, hence the subject of the embedded sentence can not be substituted for *it*. Since under this hypothesis the subject of the embedded sentence ends up in the matrix sentence with *expect* but not with *hate,* we can test this hypothesis by seeing whether it accords with the facts of reflexivization. As Lees and Klima (1963) have shown, the reflexivization transformation applies only within a single S. If the hypothesis sketched above is correct, then reflexive pronouns should be grammatical in the position of *Lucille* in (81c), but not in (80a) or (80b). And this is the case. The sentence

(86)   Fred expects himself to be nominated.

is perfectly grammatical. But sentences like

(87)   a. *Fred hates it for himself to be nominated.
           b. *Fred hates for himself to be nominated.

are ungrammatical. The differential ability of reflexive pronouns to occur in (86) and *(87) confirms that with *expect* the embedded subject is raised into the matrix sentence, as shown in (84), but with *hate* it remains in the lower sentence, as in (85).

Having established that (84) and (85) show the correct derived constituent structure for (81) and (80) respectively,[15] we can now observe how these sentences behave under Question Formation and Relativization. In both cases, an object of *sing* can be questioned.

(88)   What do you expect Lucille to sing?

(89)   a. What do you hate it for Lucille to sing?
           b. What do you hate for Lucille to sing?

But if we try to question a noun phrase in the position of *Lucille* in these sentences, the resulting sentence is grammatical in the case of *expect,* but not in the case of *hate.*

(90)   Who do you expect to sing Dixie?

(91)   a. *Who do you hate it for to sing Dixie?
           b. *Who do you hate for to sing Dixie?

Since in the dialect under discussion *for* never deletes with *hate,* the sentence

(92)   *Who do you hate to sing Dixie?

is also ungrammatical. The ungrammaticality of *(91), which would otherwise be a strange aberration, is explained by the surface structure constraint (9). When a noun phrase in the position of *Lucille* in (85) is moved out of the embedded sentence, an S is left behind which does not contain a subject.[16] The constraint (9) will therefore reject the sentence as

---

15 Note that the appearance of the infinitive in the embedded sentence in (80) can not be accounted for by means of the Kiparskys' proposal discussed in Chapter One, according to which the infinitive appears when the subject has been removed from an embedded sentence. In (80), as I have taken pains to show, the subject has not been removed, and yet the complement verb is in infinitival form. This is also the case in sentences like (58). If the Kiparskys' proposal is correct for English, then, there must be more than one source of the infinitive.

16 An important question which has not been answered here is this: Why isn't the embedded S-node in (85) pruned when the subject NP is moved out of the complement sentence? If this S-node is pruned, (9) will not reject *(91) as ungrammatical.

One possibility might be to attempt to preserve Ross's condition that S-nodes that do not branch are pruned by making crucial use of the *for* in (85) to prevent pruning. Perhaps such a proposal could be made to work.

It is striking in this connection that Ross provides no evidence from English that

ungrammatical. In the case of (90), however, the noun phrase that is questioned is in the matrix sentence, as shown in (84). Moving this noun phrase out does not leave an S without a subject, and the sentence is grammatical. The derived constituent structures (84) and (85), which were motivated on independent grounds, together with the surface structure constraint (9), which is also independently motivated, automatically predict the difference in grammaticality between (90) and *(91).

---

removal of the subject of an embedded S, whether by Equi-NP Deletion or by It-Replacement, causes pruning of the embedded S-node. Pruning has been assumed to take place in such cases because of Ross's general condition that S-nodes that do not branch are pruned. But pruning actually creates a problem in these cases, because sentences like

(v) I believed Bill to have recommended me.

and

(vi) I forced Bill to recommend me.

must be prevented from becoming

(vii) *I believed Bill to have recommended myself.

and

(viii) *I forced Bill to recommend myself.

respectively. In the latter case, Equi-NP Deletion can be ordered after Reflexivization, so that pruning will not occur until after Reflexivization has applied. The Ordering Strain Principle to be discussed in the Epilogue suggests that a solution that does not depend on crucial ordering is to be preferred, and the ordering solution just proposed runs into difficulty in the light of examples like

(ix) *Sally thinks I forced Bill to recommend myself.

in which the ordering of Equi-NP Deletion after Reflexivization does not prevent Reflexivization from applying on the third cycle. Ordering Reflexivization after It-Replacement to prevent *(vii) from being generated would run into exactly the same difficulty. What is worse, precisely the opposite order is needed to account for the reflexive pronoun in

(x) I believed myself to have been recommended by Bill.

These examples should make it clear that it is not obvious that removal of the subject of an embedded S causes the dominating S-node to be pruned in English.

The evidence that removal of an embedded subject causes pruning of the dominating S-node is based on the phenomenon of clitic placement in Serbo-Croatian discussed in Browne (1968) and Ross (1967b). If it should turn out that Equi-NP Deletion causes pruning in Serbo-Croatian but not in English, and that there is no structural difference between the analogous sentences in the two languages to which this difference in pruning can be attributed, Ross's proposal for a universal pruning convention will have to be abandoned.

Another way of attempting to prevent pruning in *(91) would be to attempt to develop a theory of pruning according to which the removal of an embedded subject by some rules, but not others, causes pruning of the embedded S-node. Hopefully, it would be possible to show that the assignment of rules to the pruning-causing or non-pruning-causing class is not arbitrary, but predictable, perhaps as a function of their ordering or of whether or not they are cyclical.

The claim that (9) automatically accounts for the ungrammaticality of *(91) de-

Nothing has been said here about the level of derivations at which the constraint (9) applies. Since it may be difficult to identify the subject of a sentence after certain late transformations such as subject-verb inversion in questions and various stylistic reordering transformations have applied, the constraint (9) may have to apply at some level prior to final output. The interesting question of whether there is some such level as "shallow structure" at which certain constraints must be stated will be left open here.[17]

It has been my purpose in this chapter to show that there are languages that have the surface structure constraint (9) in their grammars, and that the presence or absence of this constraint in the grammars of particular languages forms the basis for a typological division among languages. The examples used have been confined to languages with which I am more or less familiar, but languages of Type B, at least, seem to be very common and widespread. I know of no languages other than French and English of Type A; the question of whether or not there are others must be left for future research.

Since languages can differ typologically according to whether or not they have the constraint (9) in their grammars, it follows that the addition of this constraint to the grammar, or the loss of it, is a conceivable form of linguistic change. The case of French shows clearly that the addition of the constraint (9) to the grammar of a language actually is possible as a form of linguistic change. Latin was a Type B language, as are the other Romance languages with which I am familiar. At some point in the history of French, then, the constraint (9) must have been added to the grammar. According to my hypothesis, once this constraint was added to the grammar, it was impossible to move the subject out of a subordinate clause, subject pronouns could not be deleted, and the various constructions that we examined required expletive subjects, as is the case in modern French.

It is not at all clear just how such a process of linguistic change takes place, and for this reason the case of French would make an interesting historical study. Under my hypothesis, it is possible for a Type B language to have expletive subjects and to lack a rule which deletes subject pronouns. As we have seen, this is the case in contemporary Dutch. It is possible that French was at some stage like contemporary Dutch in this respect, and that the constraint (9) was then added to the grammar.

This brings us to the interesting question of what it is in the primary linguistic data that leads the language-learning child to put the surface

---

pends on sentences of this type having a derived constituent structure like (85), in which the removal of the embedded subject from structures like (85) by Question Formation or Relativization does not cause pruning of the embedded S-node. The claim would be much stronger if there were a theory of pruning which predicted that pruning would not occur in these cases. In the absence of such a theory, this claim rests on the ability of (9), which has been motivated on independent grounds, to account for the class of facts illustrated by the contrast between (90) and *(91). This class of facts would otherwise be unaccounted for. If another theory is developed that automatically accounts for these facts in another way, the claim that the ungrammaticality of *(91) is due to (9) will have to be abandoned.

17 This idea was suggested by Postal (1970).

structure constraint (9) in his grammar. Otherwise put, what conditions must be fulfilled in order for the most highly valued grammar of a language to include the constraint (9)? What was there in the data of French at the relevant stage of its history that caused the constraint (9) to be added to the grammar? Whatever the answer to this question is, parallel data must be lacking in contemporary Dutch, which lacks this constraint. An explanatory theory of language must be able to answer questions of this kind.

The constraint (9) is also interesting because it shows that surface structure constraints are not confined to essentially word-level phenomena such as the order of clitic pronouns discussed in Chapter Two. Only further research can reveal the full range of phenomena that are to be accounted for by means of surface structure constraints.

One should also ask why languages should have a surface structure constraint like (9). The attempt to answer this question should lead us to inquire about why languages have surface structure constraints at all. It has been a defect of the theory of transformational grammar that in order to account for certain empirical facts it must allow transformations to perform a number of operations that make transformations an exceedingly powerful device. Transformations have so much power to add, delete, move, and permute constituents that they are powerful enough to distort deep structures far more than they actually do. Given transformations which have this kind of power, it is very surprising that surface structures do not differ from deep structures more than they actually do. This fact has been unexplained in the theory of transformational grammar. The existence of the surface structure constraint (9) may be able to give us some insight into this matter. It may well be that the output of the transformational component of the grammars of natural languages is subject to certain surface structure constraints that reject as ungrammatical any surface structure that does not "look like" a deep structure in certain respects. If this is so, transformations may in fact produce all kinds of highly distorted surface structures that do not resemble deep structures at all, but these structures are discarded by surface structure constraints and therefore do not qualify as grammatical sentences. Only those surface structures that resemble deep structures in the relevant respects would emerge as grammatical sentences. If this is correct, it remains to discover and to define precisely what the "relevant respects" are. The surface structure constraint (9) would then be a special case of a much more general phenomenon. Whereas Type B languages do not care whether each S has a subject in surface structure, Type A languages do and discard as ungrammatical any sentence in which this is not so. It would therefore not be surprising to discover that in the grammars of some languages but not others there are other surface structure constraints that require surface structures to resemble deep structures in some other way. If this is the case, such surface structure constraints may be able to explain why surface structures do not differ from deep structures more than they actually do.

EPILOGUE

FILTERING IN GENERATIVE GRAMMAR

The problem of filtering in generative grammar arises because the base component generates structures that underlie no well-formed sentences. Grammars consequently need devices that filter out ill-formed sentences. To include such filtering devices in grammars is essentially to preserve Chomsky's idea that a well-formed sentence is one which passes through the syntactic component without any violations having taken place. In order to preserve this idea in this way, it is necessary to include deep and surface structure constraints as well as transformations in the syntactic component.

Because linguistic theory must allow grammars to make use of deep and surface structure constraints as well as the filtering power of transformations, grammars are exceedingly powerful. There is too wide a range of possibilities for dealing with particular cases in natural languages. It is therefore necessary to incorporate into linguistic theory some general principles which will restrict the range of possibilities available to grammars in particular cases.[1]

Let us consider first the role of the transformational component in filtering out ill-formed sentences. In most recent work in generative gram-

---

[1] I address myself here to the problem of the availability of too wide a range of possible solutions caused by the availability of three different kinds of filtering in linguistic theory. An analogous situation, the availability of too wide a range of possible solutions due to the fact that both transformations and syntactic features are very powerful devices, is discussed by Chomsky (1970). There he attempts to develop general principles that will decide between the use of transformations and the use of syntactic features in particular cases. While Chomsky's proposals and the suggestions sketched here are totally independent of each other, they both have the effect of reducing the role of transformations in grammars.

mar, a principle of the following kind has been implicit, although to my knowledge it has not been explicitly formulated:

(1) *The Blocking Principle:*
The transformational component blocks a derivation just in case an obligatory transformation is unable to apply because of a metaconstraint on grammars.

(1) makes it impossible to state conditions on transformations that would cause a derivation to block. Without a principle like (1) in linguistic theory, it would be possible to cause a derivation to block in any of a number of ways. For example, in the examples discussed in Chapter Two in which the pronoun sequence *se se* arises as a result of the application of the spurious *se* rule, without a principle like (1) in linguistic theory it would be possible to give a blocking condition like:

(2) The derivation blocks if the spurious *se* rule applies to a pronoun sequence which both commands and is commanded by another *se.*[2]

Allowing blocking conditions like (2) would make possible many incorrect solutions in particular cases. Most important, there are no cases known where such blocking conditions are needed. In order to exclude blocking conditions like (2), the Blocking Principle (1) must be included in linguistic theory.

The Blocking Principle is in fact implicit in most work that has been done within the framework of Chomsky (1965), since in the two cases in the literature where the filtering function of transformations is actually used, this principle is in fact adhered to. In the first set of such cases, discussed in Chomsky (1965), in which there are sentences with relative clauses that do not contain a noun phrase identical to the antecedent, Chomsky proposes that what causes the derivation to block is not a particular condition on the relativization transformation, but rather a metaconstraint on grammars that requires that all deletions be recoverable. In the other case of transformational blocking in the literature, the examples discussed in Ross (1967b), an obligatory movement transformation cannot apply because the constituent that must be moved is in a structure that nothing can move out of due to a universal constraint. As a result, derivations block and sentences are characterized as ungrammatical. Both sets of examples in the literature in which transformations are used as filters, then, conform to the Blocking Principle (1). It correctly excludes blocking conditions like (2), according to which *the application of a transformation* causes a derivation to block, and reserves blocking for cases where *the inability of a transformation to apply because of a metaconstraint on grammars* causes a derivation to block.

The only attempt that has been made to use the transformational

---

[2] As Ross (1967b) has shown, the notion "both commands and is commanded by" characterizes the notion "in the same simplex sentence as."

component to block derivations in a particularistic way that does not follow from metaconstraints on grammars was Lakoff's proposal that "absolute exceptions" be included in linguistic theory. But no evidence has ever been presented to show that they succeed in capturing significant generalizations, and we have seen that the two strongest cases of absolute exceptions—the like-subject and unlike-subject constraints—simply cannot be treated as absolute exceptions for reasons of empirical inadequacy. It is significant that this filtering device that violates the Blocking Principle is empirically inadequate. The fact that this principle rules out the use of absolute exceptions is therefore another reason to include the Blocking Principle (1) in linguistic theory.

In the course of the discussion in Chapters Two through Four, at several points we were faced with a choice between handling certain phenomena transformationally or adopting a surface structure constraint. In each case, evidence was found to indicate that the surface structure constraint was the correct solution. A stronger theory of language would in many cases dictate the choice of solution. It is our task to build such a theory by providing general principles that dictate the choice of some solutions over others and by showing that the choices dictated by these principles are in fact the correct ones. The correctness of the solutions dictated by these principles is the empirical evidence that supports the principles.

At the same time, we must redress an imbalance in present linguistic theory. Most syntactic phenomena have been handled transformationally within the framework of generative grammar, since generative grammatical theory provided little in the way of alternative solutions to specific problems.[3] The addition of surface structure constraints to linguistic theory makes possible another set of solutions to many problems, and in many cases we will be faced with a choice between a transformational solution and a surface structure constraint. The existence of such choices is closely related to another problem—the fact that transformations are far too powerful and need to be constrained. In what follows we will attempt to take a tentative first step toward suggesting the means by which these two problems can be attacked simultaneously.

The literature on transformational grammar contains a number of transformations whose application is governed by certain *conditions*. For example, there are conditions of the following kinds:

(3)   *Conditions on transformations:*
   (a) An optional transformation is obligatory under certain circumstances.
   (b) An obligatory transformation is optional under certain circumstances.

---

[3] The introduction of syntactic features into linguistic theory in Chomsky (1965) makes possible nontransformational solutions of another kind. For discussion of the problem of choosing between transformational and feature solutions, see Chomsky (1970). This problem will not concern us here.

(c) There are circumstances under which a given transformation cannot apply, even though its structural description is met.

In Chapter Four, we were faced with the question of deciding whether to place a condition of type (3a) on the *that*-deletion transformation in English. This transformation is optional and relates such pairs of sentences as

(4) a. He thinks that no one will ever find him.
   b. He thinks no one will ever find him.

But it was noted that if the subject of a subordinate clause introduced by *that* is relativized or questioned, we find paradigms like

(5) a. *Who do you think that robs churches?
   b. Who do you think robs churches?

One transformational solution to the problem would be to order the *that*-deletion transformation after Relativization and Question Formation, and to make this optional transformation obligatory just in case *that* is immediately followed by a VP. This would be a condition of type (3a) on the *that*-deletion transformation. In Chapter Four evidence was produced to show that this solution is inadequate. But it would be preferable if linguistic theory ruled solutions like this one out of consideration without at the same time excluding correct solutions.

I will here tentatively propose that the following principle be incorporated in linguistic theory:

(6) *The Condition Principle:*
   When faced with a choice between two adequate solutions, one of which imposes conditions of type (3) on transformations and the other of which does not, the solution that does not impose such conditions on transformations is correct.

This principle correctly leads us to choose a surface structure constraint over a transformational solution to the problem posed by the data of (5). It also dictates the choice of the correct solution in the case of the Spanish object pronouns discussed in Chapter Two. In Spanish, we had the option of imposing a number of conditions of type (3c) on transformations. The constraint (29) of Chapter Two, which stated that the weak form of an indirect object pronoun may not be used if the indirect object is second person singular and the direct object is first person, is a transformational constraint of type (3c). In the discussion of the various ways that the clitic sequence *se se* could arise in Spanish and the various rules that could be constrained in order to prevent such *se se* sequences from arising, we considered constraining Pronominalization, Dislocation, Indirect Object Doubling, the spellout of an underlying Pro subject as impersonal *se,* and the spurious *se* rule in order to prevent *se se* sequences from arising. All of these transformational constraints are conditions on transformations of type (3c). With the Condition Principle (6) in linguistic theory, we would not have to find evidence against these alternatives, for the Condition Principle would correctly force us to adopt a surface structure constraint in preference to placing conditions of type (3) on transformations.

The Condition Principle is to be interpreted as part of the evaluation measure for syntax.[4] In the cases that have been considered here, it would lead us to adopt the correct solutions. At the same time, it reduces the power of transformations. It remains to see whether it also leads to the choice of correct solutions in other cases that have not been considered here. It is on these grounds that its inclusion in linguistic theory must rest. The evidence presented here for the Condition Principle is not sufficient for its adoption. Since progress in linguistics depends on extracting as much as possible from the grammars of particular languages and formulating general principles from which the facts of particular languages will follow as automatic consequences, it is only by proposing such general principles and testing them against linguistic data that the field can advance.

Conditions of type (3) do not exhaust the range of conditions that it is possible to place on transformations. Specifying the range of such conditions is made difficult by the inexplicitness of the notion "condition" itself. The key phrase in the conditions given in (3) would appear to be "under certain circumstances." The intuitive notion of "condition on a transformation" seems to involve a statement to the effect that whereas in the general case a transformation does one thing, "under certain circumstances" it does something else. (3) involves cases where the applicability, obligatoriness, or optionality of a transformation is variable, depending on "certain circumstances." The notion of "condition on a transformation" should also include cases where the change a transformation effects in phrase markers is variable, depending on "certain circumstances." If conditions on transformations of this sort are allowed by linguistic theory, then a number of incorrect solutions become possible. Consider, for example, the kinds of facts that are captured by the ordering of transformations. The reflexivization transformation is said to precede the transformation that deletes the underlying second person subject of imperatives in order to account for the reflexive pronoun in such a sentence as

(7)   Kick yourself.

Reflexivization applies when the underlying *you* subject is still present, accounting for the reflexive pronoun *yourself*. But as Robert Wall has pointed out, we could let the rules apply in the opposite order and still account for sentences like (7) by complicating the reflexivization transformation. The reflexivization transformation would reflexivize any noun phrase that is identical to a preceding noun phrase in the same simplex sentence, and it would also reflexivize second person noun phrases, and second person noun phrases only, if the sentence has no subject. To do

---

4 For discussion of evaluation measures in linguistic theory, see Halle (1961), Chomsky and Halle (1965), and Chomsky and Halle (1968).

this is essentially to place a condition on the reflexivization transformation that under "certain circumstances"—namely, if the sentence has no subject—it acts differently than it does in the general case. As Wall pointed out, facts accounted for by the ordering of transformations can also be stated in this way. Since this device fails to capture significant generalizations, it is necessary for linguistic theory to exclude such incorrect solutions in principle.

One way to do this would be to extend the Condition Principle (6) to include these cases. Assuming that it is possible to specify what is meant by the notion "condition on a transformation" along the lines that have been suggested here, the Condition Principle can be restated as follows:

(8) *The Condition Principle:*
When faced with a choice between two adequate solutions, one of which imposes conditions on transformations and the other of which does not, the solution that does not impose such conditions on transformations is correct.

In addition to handling the cases dealt with by (6), the Condition Principle (8) also forces us to order the reflexivization transformation before the imperative transformation rather than place a condition on the reflexivization rule.

It is quite likely, however, that the Condition Principle (8) is still not strong enough. The condition on the reflexivization transformation mentioned above, as well as other such devices, should probably be excluded in principle. We can therefore formulate an even stronger principle.

(9) *The No-Condition Principle:*
In the grammars of natural languages there are no conditions on transformations.

Assuming a specification of the notion "condition on a transformation" along the lines suggested above, the No-Condition Principle (9) would rule out conditions of type (3) as well as conditions like the one on the reflexivization transformation and thereby make the Condition Principle (8) unnecessary. Since the literature on generative grammar contains many examples of conditions of type (3), if the analyses on which they are based are correct, the No-Condition Principle (9) is false. If the No-Condition Principle is correct, on the other hand, much in past theory and practice is incorrect. For this reason, the No-Condition Principle (9) is rather speculative at this time. It is worth mentioning, however, because it may well be correct. If it is, it would constrain the power of grammars to a considerable extent. But to the extent that it would constrain grammars and thereby enrich linguistic theory, it stands in need of empirical support.

There is, incidentally, a nontrivial problem concerning the formulation of any principles such as (6), (8), or (9). In order to formulate any such principles, we must be able to distinguish *conditions on transformations* from the *structural descriptions of transformations*. Even if the structural descriptions of transformations are restricted to Boolean conditions on analyzability, as proposed in Chomsky (1965), the existence of syntactic features in linguistic theory and the fact that the structural descriptions of transformations can refer to syntactic features makes it difficult to define the notion "conditions on transformations" in a way that will prevent such conditions from being smuggled into transformations through their structural descriptions, without at the same time constraining structural descriptions in too severe a way. This situation arises as a result of the fact that syntactic features, as Chomsky (1970) has pointed out, are an extremely powerful device. If the inventory of syntactic features that can be used in grammars is not sufficiently constrained, what are essentially conditions on transformations could be stated in the form of syntactic features to which the structural descriptions of transformations could refer. The solution to this problem obviously lies in constraining the inventory of available syntactic features in an appropriate way. If we assume that this can be done, and if the notion "condition on a transformation" can be made precise, the scope of the condition principle (8) and the no-condition principle (9) is clear, and these principles can be tested empirically. If either of these principles proves to be correct, it will not only exclude incorrect solutions like the one that would order the imperative transformation before the reflexivization transformation, but by reducing or eliminating the role of conditions on transformations, it would have the effect of reducing the load of transformations in grammars. In this connection, it is worth noting that if the No-Condition Principle is correct, it would redress an imbalance in current theory. The Blocking Principle (1), which has in practice been followed in most recent work, prevents conditions on transformations from playing any role in the filtering function of transformations. The No-Condition Principle would prevent conditions on transformations from playing a role in the other functions of transformations as well.

Returning now to the problem of developing general principles that will automatically rule out incorrect solutions, we observe that the ordering of transformations can be used to "account for" certain correlations without *explaining* them. This is to some extent linked with the practice of placing conditions on transformations. For example, in the case of paradigms like (5) in English, we note that there is a correlation between the deletion of *that* and the ability to move the subject of a subordinate clause out of that clause. The question before us is how this correlation is to be accounted for. We could attempt to solve the problem transformationally by placing a condition on Relativization and Question Formation to the effect that they cannot apply to the subject of a subordinate clause if *that* has not been deleted. This solution requires us to order Relativization and Question Formation *after that*-Deletion. Another way to handle paradigms like (5) transformationally would be to make *that*-Deletion obligatory in cases where the subject of the subordinate clause has been relativized or questioned. This solution requires us to order Relativization and Question Formation *before that*-Deletion. Each of these transformational solutions, then, requires a particular order between the *that*-deletion transformation on the one hand and the Relativization and Question Formation transformations on the other. With a surface structure constraint, however, as was shown in Chapter Four, *that*-Deletion is not crucially ordered with respect to Relativization and Question Formation.

It is true that the Condition Principle (8) would lead us to reject these transformational solutions in favor of a surface structure constraint. But it still seems reasonably likely that some other principle is needed to rule out the kind of excessive use of the ordering of transformations that must be resorted to by the transformational solutions to the problem of (5) that are sketched above. On the other hand, it is clear that there are many cases for which ordering of transformations captures significant generalizations. In the case of the reflexivization and imperative transformations, for example, ordering Reflexivization before the imperative rule embodies the claim that it is not accidental that the only reflexive pronouns that occur as the object of simple imperatives like (7) are second person. It is necessary to rule out the kind of excessive use of ordering embodied in the transformational solutions to the problem of (5) that were sketched above, while at the same time permitting ordering of transformations in those cases in which it succeeds in capturing valid generalizations. In order to do this, I will attempt to develop a notion of *ordering strain*. The amount of ordering strain in a given proposed solution is defined as the number of *pairs* of transformations that are crucially ordered.[5] It is then possible to state the following general principle:

(10)   *The Ordering Strain Principle:*
When we are faced with a choice between two adequate solutions, the one with less ordering strain is correct.

The Ordering Strain Principle, like the Condition Principle (8), is a candidate for inclusion in the evaluation measure for grammars. In the case that has been considered here, that of accounting for paradigms like (5) in English, it correctly leads us to reject the two transformational solutions sketched above, which merely "account for" the observed correlation, in favor of a surface structure constraint, which *explains* it. Note that the Ordering Strain Principle could not even be seriously considered if we did not already have a principle that rules out the use of conditions on transformations, since without such a principle, the Ordering Strain Principle would incorrectly lead us to choose a solution in which we place a condition on the reflexivization transformation over one which orders Reflexivization before the imperative rule. This suggests that it may not be possible to discover universal principles individually, since they may be crucially interdependent.

---

[5] Further problems arise in the attempt to make this definition reflect what is intuitively meant by the term "strain." For example, if Rule A must precede Rule B, and Rule B must precede Rule C, we have two crucially ordered pairs of rules, hence an ordering strain of two. Now, if there is also evidence that Rule A must precede Rule C, this should *not* increase the ordering strain to three. Some way would have to be found to incorporate such intuitively correct modifications of our simplistic definition into the definition of "ordering strain."

The Ordering Strain Principle (10) also serves to prevent us from picking the wrong solution to deal with Spanish sentences like

> **(11)** Se les da los honores a los generales.
> 'Pro gives the honors to the generals,' i.e., 'The honors are given to the generals.'

discussed in Chapter Two. We must prevent *los honores* from undergoing Pronominalization to *los,* for that would produce

> **(12)** *Se les los da a los generales.

which is ungrammatical, and the application of the spurious *se* rule would convert it to

> **(13)** *Se se los da a los generales.

which is also ungrammatical. One transformational solution would be to somehow prevent Pronominalization from applying to (11). It is then necessary to prevent Dislocation from applying as well, for with Dislocation, pronominalization of the dislocated noun phrase is obligatory, and that would result in ungrammatical sentences.

> **(14)** a. *Los honores se les los da a los generales.
> b. *Los honores se se los da a los generales.

A transformational solution here would have to prevent Dislocation and Pronominalization from applying to sentences like (11)—that is, to sentences which already contain a *se* and a third person indirect object clitic pronoun. Under this solution, then, Dislocation and Pronominalization must be ordered *after* the rule which spells out an underlying Pro subject as impersonal *se* and *after* the rule which doubles the indirect object (*a los generales*) as a pronoun (*les*). With a surface structure constraint, as was proposed in Chapter Two, Dislocation and Pronominalization are not crucially ordered with respect to these two transformations. The transformational solution, then, evinces greater ordering strain. The Ordering Strain Principle (10) requires us to adopt a surface structure constraint on the order of clitic pronouns rather than the transformational solution. As was shown in Chapter Two, this is the correct solution. The fact that it is supports the Ordering Strain Principle.

The evidence given here is not sufficient to demonstrate that the Ordering Strain Principle (10) is part of linguistic theory, but it is at least highly suggestive. More important, I do not know of any cases where the Ordering Strain Principle would lead us to adopt an incorrect solution.

As was remarked above, the Condition Principle (8) and the Ordering Strain Principle (10) are to some extent interdependent. This is so because in many cases we are trying to handle transformationally a correlation that is to be explained in some other way. As in the case of the correlation between *that*-Deletion and the ability to move the subject out of a subordinate clause in English, if we attempt to account for the correlation transformationally, we must place a condition on one rule which makes it work differently, depending on whether or not another rule has already applied. For this reason, the rule on which we place the condition must necessarily follow the other one. The attempt to account for such correlations transformationally therefore necessarily leads to greater ordering strain. For this reason, the ordering strain principle succeeds in ruling out solutions under which ordering of transformations can be used to "account for" certain correlations without *explaining* them. The surface structure constraints proposed in Chapters Two and Four succeed in *explaining* the correlations which the ordering of transformations does not.

Since the Condition Principle (8) and the Ordering Strain Principle (10) are to some extent interdependent, in order to establish each of them it would of course be necessary to show cases where each is necessary and the incorrect solution would not be ruled out by the other. Since my aim here is suggestive rather than definitive, I will not do that here. The Ordering Strain Principle, in particular, stands in need of empirical support. It is important to note, however, that if either or both of these principles is correct, the power of the transformational component is to that extent constrained and linguistic theory is correspondingly enriched.

The power of linguistic theory is the greater, the more it constrains the grammars of natural languages. Conversely, the more powerful the grammars that the theory allows are, the less strong is the theory that allows them. Within this context, let us consider the implications of the inclusion of surface structure constraints in linguistic theory for the power of individual grammars and therefore for the strength of linguistic theory itself. Let us contrast two linguistic theories.

> *Theory A:* Sentences have a deep structure that is semantically interpreted and contains information about grammatical relations. Transformations map deep structures onto surface structures. Surface structures are what result automatically from the application of transformations to deep structures. There is consequently no independent theory of surface structure.

> *Theory B:* Sentences have a deep structure which is semantically interpreted and contains information about grammatical relations. Transformations map deep structures onto surface structures. There are also constraints on surface structures which well-formed sentences must satisfy.[6]

---

[6] Chomsky (1955) raised the question of whether surface structure phrase structure rules are needed independently of the phrase structure rules of the base and concluded that they are not, since derived structure can be determined solely by base rules and rules of derived constituent structure. In other words, he considered both of these theories and, on the basis of the evidence then available, concluded that Theory A is correct. Although the precise nature of surface structure constraints remains an open question, I have attempted to show in Chapters Two through Four that Theory B is in fact correct.

It is clear that Theory B puts a wider range of grammatical devices at the disposal of individual grammars, for it allows them to use surface structure constraints *in addition to* the other devices available to grammars, while Theory A does not. For this reason, the addition of surface structure constraints to linguistic theory, *by itself,* allows grammars to be more powerful than they were under the theory without surface structure constaints. As a result, *if the availability of surface structure constraints is not used to restrict the power of grammars in other ways,* a linguistic theory with surface structure constraints is weaker than one without them.

The task before us, then, is to use the availability of surface structure constraints to constrain the power of grammars in other ways. This is what I have been attempting to do in formulating the Condition Principle (8), the No-Condition Principle (9), and the Ordering Strain Principle (10). These principles would be totally impossible in a linguistic theory without surface structure constraints, since their effect is to constrain the power of the transformational component by putting some additional load on surface structure constraints. If we can discover the range of phenomena that are to be handled by means of surface structure constraints and place appropriate constraints on the notion "surface structure constraint" itself, then we will have succeeded in placing considerable constraints on the notion "human language."

But the significance of principles like the Condition Principle and the Ordering Strain Principle goes beyond the fact that they shift a certain amount of the work load of grammars from the transformational component to surface structure constraints. Their true importance, if they are correct, lies in the fact that they contribute to the development of an evaluation measure that will enable us to choose between competing grammars. Without the availability of surface structure constraints, this step toward the development of this indispensable part of a substantive theory of language could not be taken.

Although it appears at first that the addition of surface structure constraints to linguistic theory results in more powerful grammars and therefore a weaker theory, the availability of surface structure constraints can be used toward the development of universal principles that constrain grammars and enrich linguistic theory to a considerable extent. Another possibilty also appears promising. Since most syntactic phenomena have been handled transformationally in generative grammar, it has been generally assumed that the way to constrain grammars is to constrain the power of transformations. But it has proved exceedingly difficult to do this and still account for the linguistic data. The addition of surface structure constraints to linguistic theory makes it possible to constrain grammars in another way. It is entirely conceivable that transformations *are* exceedingly powerful devices, but that the output of transformations is subject to surface structure constraints that drastically reduce the number of sentences that qualify as grammatical. As was observed in Chapter Four, transformations have the power to distort deep structures far more than they actually do in converting them to surface structures. I speculated that the reason that Type A languages have the surface structure constraint (7) of Chapter Four in their grammars might be connected with some requirement that surface structures resemble deep structures in certain respects; while Type B languages would require that surface structures resemble deep structures in some respects, Type A languages also require that sentences contain a subject in surface structure. If anything along these lines is correct, it is quite possible that transformations actually do produce a much larger variety of surface structures than are grammatical, and it falls to surface structure constraints to actually constrain the output of grammars, keeping it within the more narrow limits that we find in language. If this is the case, this is another way that surface structure constraints serve to constrain grammars and thereby enrich linguistic theory.

In this Epilogue, I have attempted to draw attention to the fact that the availability of surface structure constraints for use in the grammars of natural languages, although it at first seems to give grammars additional power, can be used to restrict the power of grammars in other ways. The question of whether there are well-formedness conditions which apply at other stages of derivations must be considered open.[7] If there are such well-formedness conditions on sentence structure, everything that has been said here about surface structure constraints applies to them as well. They will increase the power of grammars inordinately unless they are used to constrain grammars in other ways.

It has been the aim of this Epilogue to point out that the availability of three different kinds of filtering devices in grammars makes possible too wide a range of solutions in particular cases and thereby makes grammars much too powerful. It is therefore necessary to develop universal principles that dictate the choice of solution in particular cases. I have attempted to formulate several such principles in order to show that the availability of several different kinds of filtering makes it possible to develop universal principles that would have been unformulable without them. The particular principles proposed here will most likely turn out to be incorrect, but if their formulation here serves to focus interest on the problem of developing such universal principles and makes linguists aware that the range of filtering devices available to grammars makes the formulation of such universal principles possible, then this Epilogue will have served its purpose well.

---

[7] The deep structure constraints discussed in Chapter One can be interpreted as well-formedness conditions which filter out certain ill-formed sentences. Since they can also be interpreted as conditions on lexical insertion, however, the issue is not so clear-cut.

BIBLIOGRAPHY

Bergsland, K. (1951), "Kleinschmidt Centennial IV: Aleut Demonstratives and the Aleut-Eskimo Relationship," IJAL 17, 167–179.

Bierwisch, M., and K. Heidolph (1970), *Progress in Linguistics,* Mouton and Co., The Hague.

Brend, R. (1968), *A Tagmemic Analysis of Mexican Spanish Clauses,* Mouton and Co., The Hague.

Browne, W. (1968), "Srpskohrvatske enklitike i teorija transformacione gramatike," *Zbornik za filologiju i lingvistiku* 11, 25–29.

Chomsky, N. (1955), *The Logical Structure of Linguistic Theory,* Microfilm, M.I.T. Library, Cambridge, Mass.

———— (1957), *Syntactic Structures,* Mouton and Co., The Hague.

———— (1965), *Aspects of the Theory of Syntax,* The M.I.T. Press, Cambridge, Mass.

———— (1970), "Remarks on Nominalization," in Jacobs and Rosenbaum (1970).

————, and M. Halle (1965), "Some Controversial Questions in Phonological Theory," *Journal of Linguistics* 1, 97–138.

————, and M. Halle (1968), *The Sound Pattern of English,* Harper & Row, Publishers, New York.

Elson, B., and V. Pickett (1964), *An Introduction to Morphology and Syntax,* Summer Institute of Linguistics, Santa Ana, Calif.

Garvin, P. (1948), "Kutenai III: Morpheme Distributions (Prefix, Theme, Suffix)," IJAL 14, 171–187.

Gili y Gaya, S. (1961), *Curso superior de sintaxis española* [8], Ediciones Spes, Barcelona.

Gross, M. (1968), *Grammaire transformationnelle du français: Syntaxe du verbe,* Librairie Larousse, Paris.

Hale, K. (1967), "Preliminary Remarks on Walbiri Grammar," unpublished paper, M.I.T., Cambridge, Mass.

Halle, M. (1961), "On the Role of Simplicity in Linguistic Descriptions," in R. Jakobson (ed.), *Proceedings of the Twelfth Symposium on Applied Mathematics,* American Mathematical Society, Providence.

Heger, K. (1966), "La conjugaison objective en français et en espagnol," *Langages* 3, 19–39.

Hill, A. (1958), *Introduction to Linguistic Structures,* Harcourt Brace Jovanovich, Inc., New York.

Hockett, C. (1948), "Potawatomi III: The Verb Complex," IJAL 14, 139–149.

Hymes, D. (1955), "Positional Analysis of Categories: A Frame for Reconstruction," *Word* 11, 10–23.

Jacobs, R., and P. Rosenbaum (1970), *Readings in English Transformational Grammar,* Blaisdell Publishing Company, Waltham, Mass.

Katz, J., and P. Postal (1964), *An Integrated Theory of Linguistic Descriptions,* The M.I.T. Press, Cambridge, Mass.

Kayne, R. (1969), *The Transformational Cycle in French Syntax,* unpublished Doctoral dissertation, M.I.T., Cambridge, Mass.

Kiparsky, P., and C. Kiparsky (1970), "Fact," in Bierwisch and Heidolph (1970).

Lakoff, G. (1965), *On the Nature of Syntactic Irregularity,* Report No. NSF-16, The Computation Laboratory of Harvard University, Cambridge, Mass.

———— (1966), "Deep and Surface Grammar," unpublished paper, Harvard University, Cambridge, Mass.

Langacker, R. (1966), "Les verbes *faire, laisser, voir,* etc.," *Langages* 3, 72–90.

———— (1967) "A Note on Double-crosses in Linguistics," unpublished paper, University of California at San Diego.

Lees, R. (1960), *The Grammar of English Nominalizations,* Publications of the Indiana University Research Center in Anthropology, Folklore, and Linguistics.

————, and E. Klima (1963), "Rules for English Pronominalization," *Language* 39, 17–28.

Li, F.-K. (1946), "Chipewyan," in Osgood (1946).

Osgood, C., ed. (1946), *Linguistic Structures of Native America,* Viking Fund Publications in Anthropology, No. 6, New York.

Otero, C. (1966), "El otro *se,*" in C. Otero, *Letras, I,* Tamesis, London.

Perlmutter, D. (1970), "The Two Verbs 'Begin,' " in Jacobs and Rosenbaum (1970).

Postal, P. (1967), "Linguistic Anarchy Notes: Horrors of Identity," unpublished communication.

———— (1970), "The Method of Universal Grammar," in P. Garvin (ed.), *Method and Theory in Linguistics,* Mouton and Co., The Hague.

Real Academia Española (1931), *Gramática de la lengua española,* Espasa-Calpe, Madrid.

Reibel, D., and S. Schane (1969), *Modern Studies in English,* Prentice-Hall, Inc., Englewood Cliffs, N.J.

Rosenbaum, P. (1967), *The Grammar of English Predicate Complement Constructions,* The M.I.T. Press, Cambridge, Mass.

Ross, J. (1967a), "Auxiliaries as Main Verbs," unpublished ditto, M.I.T.

———— (1967b), *Constraints on Variables in Syntax,* unpublished Doctoral dissertation, M.I.T., Cambridge, Mass.

———— (1969a), "Guess Who," in *Papers from the Fifth Regional Meeting of the Chicago Linguistic Society,* Department of Linguistics, University of Chicago, Chicago, Ill.

———— (1969b), "A Proposed Rule of Tree-Pruning," in Reibel and Schane (1969).

Smith, C. (1961), "A Class of Complex Modifiers in English," *Language* 37, 342–365.

———— (1964), "Determiners and Relative Clauses in a Generative Grammar of English," *Language* 40, 37–52.

Stockwell, R., J. D. Bowen, and J. Martin (1965), *The Grammatical Structures of English and Spanish,* The University of Chicago Press, Chicago, Ill.

Vendler, Z. (1968), *Adjectives and Nominalizations,* Mouton and Co., The Hague.

Whorf, B. (1946), "The Milpa Alta Dialect of Aztec," in Osgood (1946).